TO INFINITY AND TURN LEFT

EXPLORING GOD'S PURPOSE FOR CHRISTIAN TEACHERS

For Ann

1958 – 2014

I miss you.

For my family

Beckie, Tom & Annie,

Lizzie & Hamish,

because I love you all dearly.

Writing a book is hard work, I've discovered, so whatever you think of the final outcome, it is a whole lot better than it would have been without the help of all these people; Tim Crow, Phill Moon, Adrian Parsonage, Henk van Sorge and Sonya Vickers and of course Lizzie Henderson and Beckie Cox. Thank you all for your encouragement, help, comments and loving service, you have made this a better book than I could have managed alone. Any remaining errors, however, are all my own work.

As a teacher and Headteacher of over 30 years, in both the state and independent sector, I have been humbled and challenged to re-consider my role in the classroom and the school; the influence I have over the children in my care and the staff I lead; and to listen to The Holy Spirit much, much more. Thank you Graham.

Adrian Parsonage, Headteacher, The River School, Worcester, UK.

I wish I had read this book before I started my teaching career. The author challenges teachers to surrender to Him fully, so that through them, almost in spite of them, pupils learn to foster hope and joy whatever the circumstances. Graham has inspired me once again. I will hear his hopeful message resonating in my mind when I train young teachers.

Sjoerd van den Berg – Teacher Trainer, Driestar Christian University, The Netherlands.

In this great book, we find ourselves walking with Graham Coyle as he walks with God and his students into the classroom, or onto the sports field, or away on a school trip. The touch is light, the language is accessible and the humour is infectious. In it all, the author's worshipful and serving heart is palpable. I heartily recommend this book for all who teach.

John Shortt, Professorial Fellow in Christian Education, Liverpool Hope University, UK.

A copy of this provocative book would be a good bedside companion or something to take with you on regular visits to a coffee shop. Graham draws on a lifetime of God turning up in his classroom, and in leading Christian educators worldwide. For every teacher who wants to deepen their understanding of the significance of what they are doing with children.

Phill Moon – Founding Headteacher, Bradford Christian School, Founder of the Essential Christian Teacher course.

Graham's humorous (and humble) reflections on his years spent teaching and leading in education, give an honest account of what is possible when we invite Holy Spirit to direct both our personal lives and our classrooms. Graham reminds Christian Educators that by choosing to live and teach out of an awareness of Holy Spirit presence, it's entirely possible that global revival through education will come in this generation.

Rachel Wilding, International Director, Kingsway School, Auckland, NZ.

If Graham Coyle's aim was to create a book that contains humour in buckets, inspiring stories aplenty and thought-provoking moments that make you stop in your tracks and challenge you to view things as God does, then Graham has been hugely successful. Highly recommend this book for those who want to keep Jesus at the centre of their lives, and learn further how to let God's love overflow into the lives of those young people they work with.

Stuart Woodburn - Head of Primary, Merchants' Academy Primary School, Bristol. A school in the area of highest teenage suicides and domestic violence in England.

I loved this book – the honesty – the sensitivity to Holy Spirit – the impenetrable faith … What a glimpse of heaven in education! With the call of teaching comes the responsibility to create a "climate of hope" and be a "voice that brings a heavenly perspective" to every child placed in your class by Father God.

Kaya Lombaard - Assistant Lead Principal of Regional Schools Pacific Hills Education Group of Schools, Australia

Rooted in his experience as a well-travelled and highly accomplished educator and leader, Graham offers Christian teachers a treasure trove of remarkable testimonies, sage advice and profound biblical insights. Taken together, these lessons will serve to inspire and clarify God's purpose for their work. With a warm, relaxed and humorous feel to his writing, in this his debut book, Graham draws the reader in and puts them at ease. Enjoy!

Garrie-John Barnes, School Inspector and former Headteacher.

I love to read stories and this book is a collection of great and real stories. Quite few times I could picture myself in the situations described. A favourite quote is about the teacher whose desire was 'to see his pupils achieve far more than they ever thought possible'. It literally brought tears to my eyes, so simple, yet so beautiful. If my teachers had been like that while I was a student, the beginning of my adult life might have been very different.

Agnieszka Crozier, Vice-Chair of EurECA and Principal, Proem Christian Education Center, Poland.

This book is quite different from anything I have read about education. It is not a guidebook to become a successful teacher. It is more like an invitation to join a man on the journey of serving God and serving students during the everyday life of school. It is entertaining, challenging and inspiring.

Sven Magnusson, Educational Consultant, Swedish Christian School Council.

I love this book! Graham gives away generously his wealth of over thirty years of teaching experience - not just as anecdotes, but always tying them in artfully with biblical principles which will strengthen the vision and faith of a Christian teacher. It's about building a cathedral rather than hewing blocks of stone. It's infused with that unmistakable Coyle sense of humour which turns suspenseful reading into 'love it' reading.

Matt Kaegi, former Chair of EurECA, retired special education teacher, Switzerland.

Graham has an incredible ability to lift our eyes from the 'here and now' to what could be. In this book he is able to stir faith and expectation through his presentation of personal stories, skilfully woven together with biblical insight, which will leave you smiling, challenged and ultimately pointed towards the purpose of God for you in your educational role.

Steve Beegoo, CEO of The Christian School's Trust, UK.

TO INFINITY AND TURN LEFT

EXPLORING PURPOSE AS A CHRSITIAN TEACHER

Contents

Intro - Don't Buy This Book (For the Wrong Reasons)

If you are a teacher looking for a really helpful, step-by-step, guide as to how to be a better Christian witness through your work, this may not be the book for you. So, even though I'd be truly flattered that you'd bought this book, I'd be more upset if you were disappointed.

With that in mind let me explain what this book is really about.

It's a series of stories, most of them mine, aiming to illustrate some of the things which can happen when we truly desire to explore the possibilities of God working in our classes.

Many of the stories are about experiences which didn't work out as expected, and what I learned through them. Over the more than 30 years I've been teaching, I realise I've learned far more from reflecting on interventions which demonstrated God's wisdom and ability, than I ever have through being impressed with my own.

The chapters are short and designed to be read when you might have a few spare moments, perhaps whilst enjoying a coffee, or towards the end of the evening. They also each have a reflective question at the end. These are to try and help you apply what you've read to your own life. They may not all fit you, but I hope that some of them will.

In addition, there are some chapters which have a more 'devotional' style. These are there to help you engage personally with the Word of God, and of course with God Himself. The whole premise of the book is that God wants to be involved with you in an exploration of His purpose for your life. This doesn't happen without some effort on your part, so every now and then I suggest that you hit the pause button, and give yourself to this adventure.

I've spend a lot of my time praying and working towards a goal. The goal of seeing more of us as Christian teachers, become more captivated by knowing Jesus is with us in our classrooms, all day, every day. It's my conviction that we could see our classes, schools and nations transformed through this, which seems pretty amazing really.

So, I hope that you enjoy the book. I hope that you enjoy it so much that you tell others about it. Mostly though, I hope the book has the effect of leading you further along your own exploration of God's purpose for you as a teacher and a releaser of His great purpose in others.

Use Your Imagination

Imagine the world in fifty years' time. Dream a bit about what it might be like. Imagine cancer is such a rarity when it does develop, it no longer holds the same level of fear because it can be treated so effectively. Imagine we have moved so far along the road of dealing with climate change that it is as much a part of history as gas street lighting. Imagine we have seen social media develop to such a degree that it is common for all outlets to be dominated by stories of good news, of people being kind and generous and demonstrating acceptance and hospitality to those previous generations ostracised and vilified.

Take a little time to dream about these things. What else can you imagine? Crime drastically reduced, the instance of mental health problems significantly lessened, technology radically enhancing the lives of those with disabilities? What about economics? Imagine a society where the poorest have better housing, healthcare and nutrition and where the richest have a greater sense of gratitude and responsibility. Imagine if the arts and the media were praised for their positive impact in the world rather than criticised for something else.

What about education? What if education worked in such a way that it prepared young people to live knowing what they knew could make a difference to others? What if places of education, at any level, were filled with teachers of such joy, ability, wisdom and courage that they set out to train worldchangers knowing they were born to do just that?

Why all this imagining? Because if you are a teacher reading this right now, you are a visionary. You have to be because your role, your calling, requires it of you. At the outset of every academic year you have to have a vision of where you are taking your pupils to and some kind of belief you and they will arrive, hopefully together and in one piece.

Yes, you have plans, schemes and strategies which will take you on this journey step by step, lesson by lesson, but you are the visionary and you can see that there is a goal, there is a purpose. So when you get asked, as I have been on many occasions, 'Sir, is there a point to this?' you can say, 'yes' with conviction and, if there is time, you might even be able to explain what the point is.

I remember one particular outdoor education trip to Snowdonia in North Wales. We were planning to do some orienteering in the afternoon in a forest area with a beautiful lake at its centre. We hiked uphill along forest tracks which were all quite enclosed but I knew the scene opened out at the top where the lake was. There were around fifteen pupils aged fourteen or fifteen plus staff. The idea was to have lunch at the lake and then use it as a base to follow the orienteering route in the afternoon. One of my aims though was to help my pupils appreciate the beauty of their surroundings and to have some reflective time to make the most of being where they were. I didn't try to be over-ambitious, one minute of considered silence was about all I had hopes for and I thought it best to do that at the lake immediately before lunch.

We arrived and I announced my plan before they had a chance to sit down and tuck in. I said I'd time them for one minute and suggested that they just stood, looked and listened; then they could eat.

They were brilliant. In the silence, broken only by the sound of the breeze and the occasional bird, they looked around and took in all that the scene could offer them. They had almost made it to one minute and to be honest I was pretty pleased with the whole exercise.

Among the group was a lovely young guy who could cause his fair share of disruption and was not noted for his capacity to wonder at the natural surroundings, but he was liked by all including me. At around 58 seconds, with a characteristic grin, he piped up and asked a brilliant and perfectly timed question: 'Is a minute up yet, Sir?'

It broke the silence but made the moment. I laughed, the group laughed and the lad just smiled. I have no idea how well the occasion is remembered by any of the group, but I'm certain what I had asked of them had to do with imagining. There was purpose in the silence, a purpose much more significant than the exercise itself. Perhaps they couldn't grasp it at the time but it didn't matter too much. I simply wanted to help my group begin to see something bigger, further and beyond them, even though all they wanted to do was eat lunch.

If teaching is about anything it is about helping people into what is currently beyond them.

What is God's desire for you as a teacher? There are numerous books, conferences and courses that will give you part of the answer. For me though, there is something fundamental to grasp which I don't hear talked about nearly as often as it should be. If we as teachers don't have something to lead our pupils into, then where are we going?

When Jesus called his disciples He said 'Follow me'. He was going somewhere and He invited them to go with Him, to join Him on the journey. What is more, He invited them to become something which they were not yet. He saw something they did not perceive, because

19

He was looking into a realm or dimension they had yet to become aware of.

The relationship between you and your pupils is not the same as with Jesus and the disciples, but I believe God's love for them is the same as it was for the disciples and therefore His desire to reveal Himself through you is as strong as it was with Jesus.

I hope this book will help you to become more aware of God's purpose for you and His purpose for your pupils. I hope it will give you a greater awareness of a realm where you can discover vision and uncover resources to help you guide your pupils into their destiny as worldchangers.

Remember the world that you were imagining in fifty years' time? Why shouldn't the doctors, economists, carers, ecologists, entrepreneurs, artists, mothers and fathers responsible for those changes be in your class now? Who is to say that God does not have such a purpose for your pupils? Who is to say you cannot help them on their journey?

Imagine again, just for a moment. Imagine standing in God's presence one day, your race having been run. Imagine Him showing you all the impact of your service and sacrifice, and of exactly how Heaven and Earth were changed because of how you had walked through your life with Him.

If you don't imagine it now, you might not recognise it when it comes.

I hope this book will help you imagine.

To think about – what can you imagine as long-term outcomes from your teaching?

Doing a Good Job

Most of us just want to do a good job, don't we? We just want to know that all our efforts, all our preparation, teaching and follow-up is doing our pupils some good, but how do we know? It's not easy to measure. Yes, there are exam results, tests and the like but I have never found those particularly helpful for me to know how I'm really doing as a teacher. Measurements of any sort rely on some kind of standard scale and so inevitably carry an inherent comparison with others. The internal questions I have are not answered by those types of comparisons. I'm not looking to be the best of a bunch, I want to know how I'm doing in regard to being the best that God has created me to be. What I want to know is am I serving well, am I making the best of what I've been given, am I helping my pupils at a personal level as they spend time in my class, am I sowing something into their lives which God can use in their futures? In short, am I making my Heavenly Father happy?

Jesus told a story of servants given different amounts of money to look after whilst their master was absent (Matthew 25:14-30). During his absence they worked with their resources to bring increase, to make a difference. The faithful servants used their skills and wisdom well and were rewarded whilst the fearful, lazy servant didn't and wasn't. Notice the faithful servants understood their master's wishes and therefore had a basis to work from, whereas the other's fear limited him in how he operated. Ultimately this led to a bad end for him, all because of a lack of understanding of what he had been entrusted with and why.

The tale tells me that if I want to know how I'm doing in fulfilling a responsibility, I need to be able to answer these questions.

Do I truly understand the underlying purpose?

What resources have I been given?

What is my relationship with the person who has given me this responsibility?

I spent a lot of my time teaching physical education and I loved almost all of it, so you'll have to forgive me if I use a lot of PE stories and analogies. In this case though it's entirely apt.

It was a compulsory subject but not one that most followed through to an examination level. This meant across any given class the measures they were assessed by could become fairly subjective. So, if my attention became overly focussed on achievement through success in exams, I think I'd have missed the point of why I was there. I might also have missed some of the most rewarding and entertaining moments from my lessons.

One exercise I enjoyed from time to time was to let the pupils invent a new game. The object was to help them see that agreed structure, boundaries and conventions were important if everyone was to participate in an activity on a fair and relatively equal basis. I stipulated the items of equipment to be used and the space available along with some other general parameters.

On one occasion a mixed group of fourteen year olds ended up with a game involving an old, slightly deflated football being kicked, thrown and caught by two teams between two simple goals about thirty metres apart. Players were not allowed to run with the ball nor to make physical contact with opponents but they could harass and intercept any passing or catching. Initially the game lacked a name but inspiration came from a somewhat dramatic young lady who was being very effectively prevented from passing by about six opponents. She suddenly screamed out, 'you're all snapping around me like piranhas!' and so the game of 'Piranha' was born.

You see, my chief goal was not to see my pupils achieve the top grades, or even to become the most skilled performers. No, my chief goal was to see them grow in confidence in the activities concerned and enjoyment at whatever level was right for them as individuals. Play is important to us as God's creations. I believe it is a gift from Him. So it made sense to me that my aim in teaching these activities needed to be somehow aligned to God's purpose. If I, as a child of God, enjoyed physical activity then it seemed reasonable others could do the same if I led them wisely and sensitively.

My treasured moments from thirty years of teaching PE were more often found in the look of satisfaction on the face of a young pupil who, after many, many, many attempts, finally managed to master a basic skill, than in the grade they received for doing it. Please understand I'm not against exams and grading, what I am against is those things being regarded as the sole measure of personal achievement for teachers who have set their hearts to represent Jesus to their pupils.

I've always had a strong suspicion there were frequent moments of play with Jesus and His disciples. I can't prove it but I find it difficult to believe it didn't happen. It probably wasn't football or basketball but I've little doubt whatever form it took, it happened. If it was important for Jesus then, it must still be important to Him today.

Let's return to the parable. My understanding of God's desires for people will impact on my motivation and actions if I am shaping an activity for them. The internal and important questions of my heart will get more satisfactory answers if I know what the real task is. This is not to belittle the more obvious, external issues relating to my duties as an employee of a school or system, but it does give them context and prevents them from becoming the be all and end all of my work in teaching.

To think about – are the measures you are using to tell you if you are doing a good job the same ones the Lord uses?

How Did We Get Here?

Don't you find that the Bible is remarkably unhelpful on some topics? Is it ok to watch this TV programme? Are tattoos evil? Should I buy more organic food? Who should I vote for? Scripture is silent on the specifics of all of these and much more besides, including a lot to do with education. The reason is because we have been given direct access to the Holy Spirit who has promised to help us when we don't know what to do. Things aren't specifically written out for us because, if they were, we wouldn't bother to search for insight and understanding. Asking, seeking and knocking are activities Jesus seems to recommend to us (Matthew 7:7).

As far as education goes, this has meant the responses Christians have come up with through the years have varied considerably.

Hundreds of years back there was very little in the way of education at all. Few people could read or write and most didn't need to. It was far more important they were skilled in the things that would keep them alive such as killing wolves and bears or growing food. Almost all of these involved hard manual labour but not much reading or writing. Among the few who were literate were the monks and priests and they began to educate people so that they could pass on the skills to accomplish priestly and monkly duties such as reading Latin, copying manuscripts and a whole range of other useful things. Christians were educating but it was fairly restricted at the time to a small percentage of the population.

Shooting forward into the 18th Century one of the spin-offs from the awakening and growth of the Church in the UK through the ministries of Wesley, Whitfield and others was the care shown for a changing society affected by the Industrial Revolution and the rapid growth of cities. Christian reformers saw literacy was now increasingly important and not just because it would enable people to read the Bible. At first through individuals such as Robert Raikes and even Charles Wesley himself, but later on through parish priests and concerned Christians across the land, schools were established and it became more common for children to receive a basic education.

Initially the British government were not so enthusiastic about this. They had seen the devastating impact of the French Revolution and were convinced it was largely a bad idea if people could think, read and write for themselves. The last thing they wanted was for an educated population to realise that they could probably do a better job of running the country than the politicians were. However, as time went on and revolution didn't occur, they began to see the economic and social value of an educated workforce.

They changed their approach and offered the churches money to build new schools as long as the churches supplied the teachers and the curriculum. In many respects this was a very good deal, but it ran into a tragic but perhaps inevitable obstacle. The two main branches of the church, the Church of England and the Free Churches, could not agree upon certain matters of doctrine or catechism which would be taught in the schools. The delay caused by this wrangling held up the development of the church schools and the government got fed up waiting. Having decided universal education was a good idea they, not surprisingly, wanted to get on with it. The result was they took control themselves and the church lost the opportunity to be more involved at such a significant level. To use a sporting analogy, as the church, we dropped the ball.

As a church our history in education is we have sometimes struggled to get the balance right between being effective for the Lord and honouring the state. Is it possible we can teach in a way which enables us to have integrity before both? I believe it is when we understand God's desires for us and the incredible ways He has to implement them.

As an example, the majority of my teaching experience has been in a small sector of the British education scene comprised of independent, evangelical Christian schools. It was one of many starting from scratch. We had minimal funding and we lacked experience in running schools. What we did have in abundance though was enthusiasm, a willingness to make sacrifices and devotion. We were working hard to get things afloat and then keep them there. On occasion though, I believe this gave me an unbalanced and incorrect perspective on what the rest of the church was doing in education, which I regret to say I often didn't see clearly enough. Consequently I missed the fact that there were many other Christians from different backgrounds and traditions who had much to teach me and might even have wanted to learn from what I had been doing.

Thankfully things have changed a good deal and so have I.

It's a bit like climbing a mountain. There are many different routes that can be taken and in the ascent we can sometimes lose sight of where we are going. We may also not realise there are others who are climbing who we won't encounter at all until we get nearer to the top but isn't it true that as we climb higher we become closer to each other and see each other more clearly?

Thousands of you as dedicated Christians are working really hard to bring the life of Jesus into your schools and classes. We are working in different educational settings, but should be heading in the same direction because we are following the same Jesus, and He is only going one way. Our ways of following Him in education can look different but what we desire to see as outcomes for our pupils can be exactly the same.

To think about – can you see beyond what you are doing to see what God is doing?

Why Exactly Are Your Pupils There?

I have often asked this question whilst teaching but never aloud of course. It seems to me there are many possible answers, each with varying degrees of depth. Firstly, the state say that they need to be. They have to learn somewhere or they won't be able to live in the modern world or get a job, and they happen to live near to the school or their parents have chosen the school for some other reason. All this is true of course and applicable in the vast majority of cases.

A different type of answer lies with your specific task in the school. They are in front of you because you teach something they need to gain skills in; writing, reading, maths, sheep shearing, whichever. This answer may be bit more satisfying than the previous one but it doesn't really excite me personally because many people can teach those skills at some level; except perhaps the sheep shearing.

If I was feeling particularly confident when asking myself this, I might answer by saying these pupils are here because I am a good teacher. I have skills, experience, qualifications and a reputation for being able to teach reasonably well. These young people will benefit from being in my lessons because they will not only learn but they may also enjoy themselves in the process. This might sound a bit egocentric to you, but truly I believe that we need to have a positive assessment of ourselves and our abilities. Not an over-estimation, just a realistic and healthy one.

However, I still don't think this is the most profound reason why a group of children or young people are in front of you or me. I think it is to do with the sovereign choice of God. I know there are the forces of government policy, parents' choices, your own life and career choices, as well as a good helping of the apparent randomisation of birth dates, parents' house-buying decisions and demographic influences. I recognise that all of those and more are factors in this but the activity of the ruler of the Universe must be understood to be above, behind and beyond all of this.

Consider yourself. You are an individual who at some point in your existence has made a conscious decision to turn control of your life over to the all-powerful, undisputed and completely loving, eternal Father of all and, even though you made the decision about it, you have also come to realise it was His initiative in the first place. He oversaw your development as an unborn child which even your mother couldn't observe (Psalm 139:13), He has taken great care over you through each stage of your life (Psalm 121:8), He saw that you were completely and hopelessly lost and heading in the wrong direction with no future or hope, and sent Jesus to rescue you (Luke 19:10) and He has shown you that He is committed to you living in the very best of His divine purpose for you (John 10:10).

So, with all of His investment in you and all of His promises to you for fruitfulness and favour, now realise He has placed in front of you a group of wonderfully made, beautifully crafted, divinely appointed people. These individuals hold the potential of housing God's Spirit and you have been selected to help teach, train, influence and inspire them with the all resources of Heaven available to you. They will be mothers and fathers, friends and work colleagues, leaders and supporters and you are a significant person in their lives right at this moment and perhaps for much longer.

How do you respond to this? Is it a fresh thought or is it something which has been a bedrock motivation in your teaching for a while? If you have never really considered this idea much before, I ask that you mull it over a bit right now because I believe if more Christian teachers connected with the desires of God in this way, it would revolutionise education across the world.

Think about the major figures of the Bible. Who shaped them as children? Who saw their potential through God-inspired eyes? Who helped build their characters, demonstrated what it was to love unconditionally, forgive extravagantly and serve faithfully? Who inspired them to reach out for more than they could see? Who showed them they could trust people of integrity, and so become people others would trust? Yes, their parents were highly significant but there were many others as well. Samuel had Eli, Ruth had Naomi, Timothy had Paul and the disciples had Jesus.

We are called to make disciples of the nations (Matt 29:19) and nations grow through classrooms.

You are called into a role where you are an influencer and you have the capacity to bring great influence for the Kingdom of God.

Consider King David. Before he became king of anywhere he was having some real problems with Saul, so he did the sensible thing and ran off to hide in a cave. The word got out and pretty soon about 400 other characters, who also had grievances with Saul for one reason or another, came to join him. We don't know exactly how David reacted to this at first but I can imagine it was with a mixture of emotions. On the one hand he might have been pleased to discover he wasn't the only one having a few issues with Saul but on the other hand he could have been forgiven for thinking 'who are all of these losers and what am I supposed to do with them?'

He did something right though because much later on we read about the exploits of 'David's mighty men' (1 Chronicles 11). Somehow, out of this collection of misfits and malcontents there emerged a group of leaders and warriors who have been renowned throughout history for their bravery and character.

One particular story is very revealing. David asked for a drink, not because he was thirsty but because he was homesick. What he really wanted was water like his mother used to give him. Can you imagine the conversation in his head?

'I'm sick of living in a cave and I'm sick of being on the run from that … from that …. well I'm sick of being on the run. What I wouldn't give for some of that cool, sweet water that we used to get in Bethlehem. Man, they don't make water like that anymore. But it's too far and I can't go because I'm stuck here in this cave with these guys.'

Of course his men didn't hear all of that, they just heard, "Oh, how I would love some of that good water from the well by the gate in Bethlehem." (1 Chronicles 11:17) but it was enough to send three of them off to get some.

When they returned with the gift of water they had risked their lives for, David was so deeply moved that he couldn't bring himself to drink it. Instead he did the best that he knew how to do and poured it out as an offering to the Lord (see Genesis 35:14). He sanctified it because of the deep love which had been the motivation for bringing it to him.

My point is this, David simply expressed a longing. He wasn't giving an order, he was simply thinking out loud but his men decided they wanted him to have what he wished for. They had been so affected by his leadership, so shaped by it, they desired to serve in any way they could.

All teachers are leaders to their pupils in one way or another. Is it possible we could allow the Spirit of Jesus to work through our teaching in such a way that it provided intentional, spiritual leadership to our pupils on His behalf? After all, He knows them through and through, and His desire is for them to know Him in the same way. Can we believe and understand that He has chosen us as His agents for a purpose far beyond our wildest imaginings?

"Never doubt God's mighty power to work in you and accomplish all this. He will achieve infinitely more than your greatest request, your most unbelievable dream, and exceed your wildest imagination! He will outdo them all, for his miraculous power constantly energizes you." (Ephesians 3:20 TPT)

To think about – what type of influence has God given you as a teacher?

To Infinity and Turn Left – Telling Your Best Story as a Christian Teacher

I hope that you are familiar with Buzz Lightyear. If not then I feel you may have missed out on one of the great characters of intergalactic literature. For the sake of the 1 in 50,000 of readers who might never have seen any of the Toy Story films, Buzz Lightyear is a space ranger who at the start of the story doesn't know he's a only a toy. He genuinely believes he's an intergalactic law enforcer, doing battle against the evil emperor Zurg.

The film makers initially named Buzz 'Lunar Larry' but they soon saw sense, and realised that nobody would take him seriously with a name like that, least of all the evil emperor Zurg. They played around a bit and came up with 'Buzz' from Buzz Aldrin, the second man to step onto the moon and considered to have the coolest astronaut name ever, and 'light-year' because it was a commonly known space term. So, Buzz Lightyear was born and aren't we glad that he was?

For a character like Buzz to stick his chin out and boldly declare 'to infinity and beyond', is as heroic as it is nonsensical, but his words genuinely match his aspirations.

Toy Story is a children's film made for grown-ups. It helps us to reconnect with the dreams and hopes that we had in our youth.

What were yours? Mine included playing rugby or basketball for England, being a pilot, working as a checkout assistant in our local Cash and Carry (ok, so I was very young then, but it seemed exciting) and driving racing cars. Strangely being a teacher never featured in any of those dreams. However, I clearly remember saying to God one day as a teenager, I don't mind what I do, I simply want to make a difference, I want my contribution to count. As far as I could see at the time, being a teacher didn't tick any of those boxes.

If we want to release the power of dreaming and imagination into others, it needs to operate in us first, but such talk is simply foolish, isn't it? How can teachers be expected to be the dreamy ones? We are supposed to be the level-headed, task-focussed, plan-orientated adults who bring balance, common sense, security and direction to our charges. Wasn't this why we went to get degrees? Are we all supposed to be like the Robin Williams character in "Dead Poets' Society"? I mean that didn't exactly end well, did it?

Somewhere there must be a balance in this. I wonder if Jesus managed it.

He was in a boat with His disciples one day and they were heading out across a lake. A storm blew up and the disciples thought Jesus should be showing a bit more concern for them, seeing as how He was literally asleep in the boat. They woke Him to say, 'Hey, we think we're going to die and you don't seem very bothered'. He dealt with the storm and showed just how concerned He was for their continued learning by telling them, 'Do you realise you could have done that?'

On another occasion they were surrounded by hungry people with next to no food so He instructed the disciples to feed them. There were only a few thousand after all. What did they think, 'You must be joking, Jesus'? In the end though, they played a significant part in the outworking of the miracle despite their low expectations.

How about when, while still in their training period, He sent them out to heal sick people, restore lepers to wholeness, deal with demonic influences and tell people all about God's good news? He was dreaming again, wasn't He? Surely it wasn't realistic to expect so much from barely prepared trainees?

You see it's like this, I think Jesus has big dreams for us.

I never expected to be a teacher, in fact I didn't even want to be one. While I was still at school my Headmaster said to me one day, 'Graham, I think you'd make a good teacher'. Well, it was news to me and to be honest, it felt like a bit of an insult. The image of teachers I had acquired by the age of seventeen did not thrill me greatly.

This was with the exception of David Wilson. If I was asked for my favourite teacher it would have to be him. He was my long-suffering music teacher who never taught me a single lesson beyond the age of thirteen but he did run the school choir, of which I was a member. On the surface he was a respectable, middle-aged, middle-class guy in a sports jacket with leather elbow patches, who played the piano and the double bassoon; but he had a hidden secret. He had the most unrealistic, unreasonable and un-dissuadable belief that his choir could rival the angelic host for the beauty of their singing. The problem was, he knew he was right and the energy he brought to his pursuit of such 'dreamy imaginings' was infectious. Somehow under his tutelage, we performed the most incredible pieces with great skill. It was a joy to be a small part of Dave Wilson's world, and had I displayed any ability and will power to become musically accomplished, my entire career might have turned out differently.

Here's the thing though, I did catch something from him and it was this, the desire to see other people achieve more than they ever thought was possible.

What I see in Jesus is He was doing the same thing and was able to bring the perspective of Heaven into the equation. He had dreams and desires for His disciples. 'Here you are Peter, James, John etc., here's an impossible situation, what are you going to do with it? How are you going to access the resources of the Kingdom of God to enable change in these people's worlds? It can be done because this is the Father's desire for you, in the power of His Spirit and using your unique mixture of gifts, working through your individual personality.'

We can have the same desires for our pupils, but to do it we have to be dreamers and we have to be visionaries ourselves. If we are not, what are we leading our pupils into?

Hang on a minute, I hear you say, there are at least two problems you are not dealing with Graham. Firstly Jesus' disciples chose to follow Him and secondly, how can you talk about leading pupils into God's desires for their lives if they have no relationship with God?

Great questions, glad you asked them.

In response to the first, our relationship with our pupils, of any age, isn't the same as it was for Jesus and the disciples. There are obvious and important differences, and I'm not going to try and draw close parallels. However, remember that in the same way He initiated the selection of Jesus' disciples, your pupils are there because the Father chose them to be in your class. Think about that for a moment.

The second question might seem a bit more challenging, because the vast majority of pupils do not appear to have any relationship with Jesus at all. How can they enter into God's story for them? My answer is this, they are already in it. They may have no perception of it at all but you, God's precious child, are their teacher. This is the strongest indication that He is already making a way for them to enter their own 'God story'. He has already sent His best answer for them, and it's you.

It all sounds like a great story to me.

To think about – what type of story is your teaching telling?

Ski Story

You may have never led a school ski trip but in many ways they are much like other trips, except with more snow. There is a long period of careful preparation with mounting excitement from the participating pupils. They earn and get given money to pay for the trip through the preceding months and you have meetings with their parents to explain what will happen and to emphasise three things: safety, safety and safety.

On one particularly memorable trip some years ago now, all started well. The travel worked out fine, a four hour coach journey, a two hour ferry and then another twenty hours' coach journey which everyone enjoyed immensely, once they had worked out the most comfortable sleeping positions.

Eventually we arrived, got established in the hotel, had our evening meal and then headed off to get the kids kitted out with their skis, boots and poles. We rose the next morning for breakfast and their first experience on the slopes. This bit was always huge fun as a group of novice, British school children navigated the snow and ice whilst grappling with oversized, unfamiliar equipment and trying to remember all the extra things that they needed such as ski pass, hat, gloves, sun cream, lip salve, goggles, money, lunch and on and on and on.

Everything went well that day, the sun shone, there was much falling over, much laughter and nobody got hurt. It had been a good day. I was delighted and relieved. The evening came and they were all in high spirits. We had a short meeting after dinner and then, with no activities planned, there was time to relax and rest as it had been a busy couple of days.

One of the lads on the trip from my own class was, like most fourteen year old boys, full of energy and rarely listened to advice. He was rushing down the stairs that evening and, as he reached the last one, he tripped and fell awkwardly, badly spraining his ankle. I was called for immediately to deal with the disaster, because it's what teachers do, right?

He was in great discomfort and, having spent a lot of my life in and around sports I'd seen a lot of injuries so I was pretty certain this one had put him out of action for the week. I was really disappointed as I also knew he had worked hard to earn and save the money throughout the preceding year. He was there with his friends and had been so excited as he had never been abroad previously. Perhaps most importantly his desire to conquer the slopes was immense but now all he could look forward to was sitting around for the rest of the week. It was bad news all round.

Frankly, it just made me angry at the unfairness of the whole situation. It simply should not have been this way. I had been expecting another, trouble free ski holiday and give my students a wonderful experience. Now this lad's whole holiday was ruined. I needed to do something. It was too late to take him to the doctor's and, whilst we had good first aid available, I had something else in mind. I said, 'Let's pray and believe God will sort this out.'

Now, please understand I was teaching in a school with a strong Christian ethos, and there was a general acceptance of praying for people and I was at liberty to do it quite openly. What didn't always happen was the prayers being answered in demonstrable ways. You may not have such liberty in your situation, but I encourage you now, your Heavenly Father is able to work in far more ways than you can imagine and so do not believe that He cannot and will not work in and through your circumstances.

We were joined in the room by one of his friends and another Christian teacher. We prayed for about ten minutes, at the end of which I invited him to try out his ankle to see if anything was different. Nothing was, it was just as painful and he could not put any weight on it. We returned to praying for another ten minutes. I invited him to do the same again and this time he was able to take a bit of weight on his damaged leg, not much, but there was clearly some improvement. However, his ankle was still badly swollen which would have made wearing a ski boot impossible.

We prayed again. This time it was different. I watched, amazed, as the swelling around his ankle reduced by ninety percent in a few minutes. He could feel something was going on and he didn't need inviting to try it out. At first he stood and then he jumped up and down and could not believe the difference from a little earlier. It was very special and we were overjoyed that God had fulfilled His promises and this lad would be able to enjoy the rest of his holiday.

He skied the rest of the week like a typical teenage boy and without discomfort. He is now the pastor of a local church as well as a successful business owner, I see him around quite often. He has seen God do many other great things but I know that he has a special memory from all those years ago.

If we want to see change in our situations we have to take risks. Change for the better rarely depends on doing what we have always done. Jesus brought change from Heaven to benefit the Earth. This meant doing things differently, establishing a changed ethos with different values and growing a culture greater and stronger than the one which existed. His attitude to women, wealth, sickness, power and religious duty all brought change and shook people up, but they also brought goodness in their wake.

As teachers we are involved with a process of change all the time and there is a real sense of us helping to provide stability for people through the natural changes of growth and education. We are aware just how much many of our pupils need certainty from us when it is often missing from other elements of their lives. What is different for us as Christians though, is that God is also involved in bringing change to us and through us. Often the change that He is aiming for is not valued by the systems within which we operate. It is because of this tension that we need His help to operate effectively.

To think about – how do you feel about taking risks with God?

Ski Story 2

The last story alone was enough to be the highlight of the trip but things did not end there. The next day there was obvious excitement in the whole group as everyone heard about the healed ankle and the kids were buzzing as we set off for the slopes. Sadly, after lunch another accident occurred. One of the girls fell off a T-bar lift on a fairly gentle slope. Normally she would have come right off and the safety mechanism on her skis would have released them from her boots. For some reason this didn't happen. Instead of her ski popping off straight away it stayed on, so one leg dragged behind her as the other was wrapped around the still-ascending lift for a few moments until it was stopped.

I was a bit further up the slope but was called back quickly. As I arrived two mountain rescue workers were preparing to take her down the slope using a sled affectionately known as the 'blood-wagon'. One was at the front of the sled and one behind, with me following. They were very experienced skiers and I was a novice so it was as much as I could do to keep up with them, and by the time I reached the bottom, the girl was already in the back of a waiting ambulance. I stuck my skis in the snow and leapt into the ambulance with her.

I recall the particular hospital we were taken to was partly staffed by nuns who wore the most bizarre and impractical head attire. Funny the details that come to mind, isn't it? Anyway, my German was, and still is, almost non-existent, but after her examination and x-rays the doctors communicated quite clearly this was the end of her skiing for the week. Bed rest and an uncomfortable trip home were all she should expect; but I was now believing for something better.

When something like this happens we have a choice about our response. For most of us an immediate reaction involves concern for our pupils, an awareness of our position of responsibility and planning of the practicalities for managing the situation with all our other concerns to attend to. Mixed up with all of this as well, if we are not careful, can be a lot of fear. Did we follow all of the correct procedures, was our planning adequate, have we covered all of the other eventualities? In short, was it our fault and are we in trouble?

These are completely understandable and can be applied to almost any situation that we as teachers find ourselves accountable for on a daily basis. Don't think for a minute these considerations didn't enter my head. They did, along with guilt from the internal accusation; 'Everything is going wrong and it is your fault'.

In times such as these we discover how we exercise faith in our professional settings. Do we have faith predominantly in ourselves and our training or do we allow God to be the one who directs and guides us through? If we do want His guidance we need to be asking ourselves two questions, what is God saying to me in this situation and how am I going to respond? I'm not proposing we set aside the procedures and responsibilities we are obligated to observe, this is simply fulfilling the requirements of our earthly job. No, I am proposing we make space in our thinking for God to lead us in a direction which will bring something different into the situation.

The disciples learned from Jesus how to do this, so when they got into sticky situations there was a model for them to follow. Paul and Silas are a great example in Acts 16. Things were going well for them on their journey with people being saved and healed wherever they turned up. In Philippi they had to deal with a young woman who was influenced by a demonic spirit. The reaction to the invasion of God's Kingdom into the city was not altogether friendly, and the two found themselves in jail. What should they do? Worship of course, what else would they do? As they focussed on Jesus through praise, they caught the attention of the rest of the prison. There was more to come though. The earthquake that followed rendered the prison fairly useless and this caught the attention of the warden.

Unlike the two other Holy Spirit-orchestrated prison breaks earlier in Acts 5 and 12, Paul and Silas didn't break out, they stayed put and led the warden and his whole household into new life in Jesus. At various points through this story there were significant choices for them to make. Do they deal with the disruption being caused by the demonically influenced girl? Do they run when the trouble starts? Do they sit dejectedly in prison feeling sorry for themselves, asking God why it's all going wrong? Do they sing quietly so that nobody mocks them, or do they, literally, bring the house down? Do they take the opportunity, again, to run when they can, or do they hang around to find out what God is going to do next? Choices, choices, choices all of the time.

We so often feel that we have no choice in matters of expressing faith in the public square, but I would suggest it is not the truth at all. What may be the truth is we need to grow confidence in ourselves in hearing, and following, the voice of God in specific situations. Especially when things do not appear to be going according to plan.

Back to the injured skier. We returned her to the hotel and I went back to the slopes to meet up with the others. As I arrived I realised something else was not right. My colleague quickly informed me another teenage boy had been involved in yet another somewhat freakish accident. Losing control on a slope he had been told not to go on, he landed head first in a snow drift. Kids, eh?

Can I just say in my defence here, and because at least two of the people on this trip are now lawyers, all of the expected safety guidelines of the time were being carefully followed! We were all really doing our best to look after this bunch, truly we were. After all, safety, safety, safety, yes?

By this stage, though, I was a little incredulous. None of this should have been happening, but after the dramatic healing the previous evening, I knew there was something else going on. When we all got back to the hotel the other teachers asked me what we were going to do. 'We're going to pray again,' I said, 'but I'm just going for a short walk first'. I went outside and began to pray on my own, I needed to get my own heart and mind correctly aligned with how God was viewing this situation. As I did so I noticed I was far from being in despair, I was beginning to pray with greater authority and certainty. I realised the Lord had delegated authority to me to deal with what was happening. The enemy had no authority to steal pleasure from these kids, and we were going to do something about it.

A release of God's action in response to prayer follows the release of authority in the son or daughter asking. We need to know that we have been granted authority to act in the situations we are placed in. We are not there by accident. If stuff is going wrong around you, don't automatically assume that you are the problem; you are probably the solution.

After about half an hour I went back inside and said to the whole group, "Ok, who wants to see someone get healed?" I was joined in the girl's room by several staff and around fifteen kids. It was packed, standing room only. The girl was sitting on her bed with her leg bandaged and supported under the knee. I told the group that we were not just there to pray for healing, we were there to see healing. I prayed briefly and invited anyone else who wanted to, to do likewise. This took around ten minutes. I then asked the girl how her knee was. God's response was as quick as it was remarkable, but it was not unexpected. She told us all she was absolutely fine now, so she got up and ran downstairs for her meal. She skied the rest of the week without any pain or difficulty and, thankfully, managed not to fall off the drag lifts any more. We later discovered a verruca on the foot of her other leg also disappeared.

Meanwhile, I didn't know what was happening with the lad in hospital. It was pre-mobile phones so I couldn't contact the staff member with him and we weren't even sure which hospital he had gone to. We prayed and trusted that God would be in complete control. A couple of hours later he was back with us in the hotel. When I asked what had happened, he told me. At one point he suddenly felt ok, he had got up from the bed and asked if he could be allowed to leave. The doctors checked him over and released him. I tried to find out what time this was, and as far as I could verify, it was around the same time we had prayed.

The impact that all of this was having on the rest of the group was astounding and beautiful. Every time someone had the slightest strain or bump they were automatically prayed for by their friends, in public. Teenagers who just a few days before were embarrassed by faith were openly demonstrating it. When they returned, all they wanted to tell their parents about were the healings. The impact of the trip was felt in the school for some months afterwards in classrooms, assemblies, lessons and local churches.

Eventually it began to wane, which was a sadness but I understood why it was difficult to maintain the same level of expectation in the normal school environment. However, it demonstrated to me what was possible when we are prepared to take God at His word. The girl concerned now has a family and they are on their second or third church plant, and the boy in the hospital has been working as an evangelist for many years. Do you think their experiences made some impression on them?

I want to add something else at this point. It's important that we keep in mind that it's not the gifts which are primarily important but the giver. "There are different kinds of spiritual gifts, but the same Spirit is the source of them all. There are different kinds of service, but we serve the same Lord. God works in different ways, but it is the same God who does the work in all of us." (1 Corinthians 12:4-6) The point I am trying to illustrate is this, I believe God gives gifts to every one of His children, but we only discover what they are and how to use them by stepping out in the situations we find ourselves in. This often involves taking risks of one sort or another. Teaching is a very risk-averse profession, and rightly so, as we have a serious duty of care towards our pupils. Therefore, we must take our risks very carefully.

Never doubt that the Lord is fully aware of your situation, and all of the factors we need to take into account in every decision we make. After all, He called you into it, didn't He? I'm convinced though, of His incredible desire to demonstrate His love to our pupils, through a multitude of ways, using a kaleidoscopic variety of gifts.

We should never disqualify ourselves, the gifts we have, or God's ability to use us where He has so lovingly placed us.

To think about – what might risk taking look like for you?

Psalm 84 for Teachers

This chapter and the two others like it are written as devotional pieces, to allow time to reflect on whatever the Lord may be saying to you. Read them differently to the rest of the book. Take a little time and allow the Holy Spirit to engage with you and reveal His truth to you. I have used different versions of the Bible for each one but feel free to use whichever suits you best.

1 How lovely is your dwelling place,
   O Lord of Heaven's Armies.

Our Heavenly Father looks at us and thinks 'beautiful, breath-taking' with exactly the same love that He had when He looked at humanity in Genesis 1 and said, 'that's very good'. An artist friend once explained to me that this was the same process artists go through in completing a great piece. They work at it until they simply know 'it is finished'.

2 I long, yes, I faint with longing
   to enter the courts of the Lord.
With my whole being, body and soul,
   I will shout joyfully to the living God.

This need not apply to Sundays or special times of worship alone, there is a desire deep in God's being which wishes us to live in the most intimate closeness to Him every day. His Spirit desires to lead us into closer communion with Him in each lesson, each playground duty and each staff meeting.

3 Even the sparrow finds a home,
  and the swallow builds her nest and raises her young
at a place near your altar,
  O Lord of Heaven's Armies, my King and my God!

Sparrows and swallows, whilst still being a part of God's creation, do not carry the significance of being made in His image as we do. We are not only welcomed but actively invited to be close to Him. Nothing brings God greater pleasure than us wanting to be close to Him.

4 What joy for those who can live in your house,
  always singing your praises.

We know that we are now the dwelling place of God rather than the Temple of the Old Covenant, we are the real, physical space the Holy One inhabits. So how does that spill out into the places where we are? Our homes, our places of work and recreation? How are we aware of being presence carriers in our schools? I have experienced times when I have been so aware of God's closeness in my classroom that it was tangible. God's desire is that there are no restrictions for any of us in knowing that He is with us wherever we go.

5 What joy for those whose strength comes from the Lord,
  who have set their minds on a pilgrimage to Jerusalem.

This is a beautiful image for us. The psalm talks of a physical, external journey to the place of security and worship in God's presence but that is related to the internal journey along pathways that are well established and well-trodden in our hearts. Other versions use the term 'set their minds or hearts on pilgrimage' which also denotes the same internal parallel. Our most epic journey with the Lord in this lifetime is this internal one which nobody else can travel but us. It's also the one that nobody else can prevent or influence without our permission. No employers, no colleagues, no parents and no pupils have the right or the authority to delay or disrupt this journey.

6 When they walk through the Valley of Weeping,
  it will become a place of refreshing springs.
  The autumn rains will clothe it with blessings.

In times of deep despair or intense pain or sorrow, we have a choice. We can choose a path that superficially lets us out of the darkness through the route of self-pity. We will often find support from friends there but we will not find the reality or depth of God's comfort. Sometimes pain cannot be avoided and we have to push into and through the pain that we experience in order to truly find the 'pleasant pool' filled from the 'brook of blessing'. It is utterly paradoxical that we should find blessing through pain. This is not to suggest that God is the cause of pain, not at all, simply that our journey with Him takes place through a fallen world.

7 They will continue to grow stronger,
  and each of them will appear before God in Jerusalem.

8 O Lord God of Heaven's Armies, hear my prayer.
  Listen, O God of Jacob.

When we travel through life in this way we cannot help but be strengthened by Him. This means that we cry out to our Father with confidence that He hears rather than in any uncertainty of His attention.

⁹ God, your wrap-around presence is our defence.
In your kindness look upon the faces of your anointed ones.
¹⁰ For just one day of intimacy with you is like
a thousand days of joy rolled into one!

When God comes up close to us we are literally overshadowed because He is so much bigger than we are. Elsewhere we are told that He overshadows us with His wings (Psalm 91:4). Have you ever considered that it might be dark in the shadow of His wings? The God who is light helping us to know we are safe and secure by bringing us into the darkness of close protection? Just like a small child snuggling up to their parent. In this embrace God looks with ultimate kindness and tenderness on us. This type of intimacy cannot be described easily, only experienced.

Thankfully we are invited right inside. There is no need for us to stay in the doorway.

11 For the Lord God is our sun and our shield.
  He gives us grace and glory.
The Lord will withhold no good thing
  from those who do what is right.

Part of the purpose of an ancient shield was to dazzle and intimidate the opposition. God's desire is to show His glory and goodness through us, we are his ambassadors. He tests our capacity to handle all that He has for us like a refiner purifies gold or silver. The more we understand this the more we can engage with the testing process. As teachers, aren't we aware of needing to test and try learners out so that they can progress to higher and greater things? The same is true for us. Let's not miss the best provision that God has for our futures by missing the lessons from the experience of the present.

12 O Lord of Heaven's Armies,
  what joy for those who trust in you.

This is not joy and peace only for the future, this is for now, for today. Our Father has made provision for us in this regard for this moment and every moment. All we need to do is to live in complete trust. "You will keep in perfect peace all who trust in you, all whose thoughts are fixed on you!" (Isa 26:3)

To think about – how has God spoken to you about your teaching through this passage?

Intimacy and Courage

Have you ever done a daft thing when in an unfamiliar place? It seems to have happened to me a lot. This particular story happened on the same ski trip as the remarkable healings but has nothing to do with healing at all. We were travelling by coach from England to a resort in the Alps. We crossed a border somewhere quite remote in the mountains, so it was quiet and extremely picturesque. Our British drivers got out to work through the paperwork which was required and the rest of us stayed on the coach. There were a couple of very severe-looking border guards around with very serious-looking hand guns attached to their belts but otherwise everything was calm and peaceful.

After a couple of minutes one of these guards came over, saw I was near to the driver's seat and began issuing instructions to me in his native tongue. This created two problems. Firstly I didn't understand at all what he was saying, and secondly, he didn't understand what I was explaining to him about me not understanding. Catch 22?

Whatever he was saying, he obviously really wanted me to understand as he kept saying it with more insistence and increased arm-waving. Now, I don't want to exaggerate this next point but I'll simply mention how convinced I became that all of this arm-waving was getting nearer and nearer to his gun. It seems irrational I know, but I have an aversion to picking fights with foreign, uniformed officials carrying firearms. It's happened on more than one occasion and so I have come to the decision to agree with their point of view.

Eventually I realised he was unhappy the coach's engine was still running and he wanted me to switch it off. Apparently, it was illegal to leave a parked vehicle on the side of a road with the engine on, and as far as he and his gun were concerned, the border post was included in that directive. Initially, I was uncertain what to do as I reasoned the drivers must have left the engine on for some good reason. However, the not-so-friendly border guard grew ever more insistent and finally, in the name of international diplomacy, I switched off the engine.

He was happy, well, well, that might be an overstatement; more satisfied that he'd got his way, so he moved off. I settled down again wondering what the selection process was like for border guards in that part of the world. The drivers returned and off we went. Or rather we didn't.

The coach wouldn't start. The coach wouldn't even turn its engine over. The coach had died. Ooops!

I immediately owned up and blamed the border guard. I explained the whole situation carefully, without a hint of hysteria, trusting the drivers would jump to the correct conclusion and see that it wasn't my fault at all.

They tried several times to start the coach with no success. They then did the sensible thing and got out to look at the engine and the electrics of the vehicle so they could enact the time-honoured ritual of scratching of heads in puzzlement. I, meanwhile, explained to the rest of the group why we weren't going anywhere and suggested they enjoy the scenery until the situation changed.

It didn't change very quickly. The drivers were at a complete loss as to why the coach wouldn't start. They tried to contact a mechanic at their firm's garage in England but it was too early for him to be at work yet and they had no home number for him; and of course, there were no mobiles yet, remember?

I then made a suggestion, couldn't we bump start the coach? Surprisingly the drivers thought this was a better idea than even I did. So I explained to the group of teenagers what we were going to do and they thought it was a truly awesome idea.

Let me clarify some things at this point. We were on a small, quiet road in the Alps. The broken down bus was blocking the border crossing, so temporarily we were an international incident. The guards were not looking enthusiastic about us staying where we were and something needed to happen quickly. In today's teaching climate I might have thought differently about it but, to be honest, it all seemed quite safe and reasonable, so the end result was we gathered at the back of the bus to try and get it started.

Surprisingly it wasn't too difficult to get the thing moving, despite there being a slight uphill gradient. Not surprisingly we were unsuccessful in starting the engine; but we had fun trying.

After another hour or so of phoning the garage, locating the relevant mechanic, further scratching of heads, finding hidden fuse boards and finally discovering the correct fuse to replace, we ventured off again to reflect on how differently they do things in other countries.

The image of God's people being strangers in another land is a powerful one. Egypt and Babylon were physical places where God's people found themselves in very unfamiliar surroundings. In the New Testament the image changes to help us understand that we are living in the same space as everyone around us but under a different authority. We switched our allegiance when we gave our lives into the hands of a loving Father, so now our hopes and expectations are focussed on a reality far greater than everything else; the reality of the Son of God (Colossians 1:13, 2:17, Hebrews 6:19).

The majority of our schools, in common with almost everything around us, are not based on the values we are embracing as citizens of the Kingdom of God. This means we have to learn to handle the difference between what we are truly living for and what is expected of us from our employment.

There is a very old joke told of a visitor to a rural region who was hopelessly lost and in need of directions. As they drove around they came across a local, standing by the side of the road. 'Excuse me please, could you help me with directions to (fill in a place name here for whichever area you wish to stereotype)?'

'Of course I can, sir,' came the reply, 'but if it were me trying to get there I wouldn't be starting from here.'

We might not choose to start from where we are, but it's impossible to move anywhere if we don't accept where we start from. In the Bible, Daniel is a fantastic example of someone who understood the difference between where he was and where he was heading.

You are probably familiar with aspects of his story, strange diets, weird dreams, supernatural handwriting, scary lions and mind-blowing prophetic visions. We sometimes become over-familiar with the details of his story and forget they are not describing the life of an average civil servant.

There are two qualities I notice about Daniel's life which go together in an irresistible and powerful combination; courage and intimacy. They were essential to Daniel to understand and overcome the circumstances surrounding him. They are equally essential to us but here is the powerful point, they have to go together, either one on its own is not effective. Courage without intimacy is just bravado and intimacy without courage is just sentimentality.

Look again at Daniel's life. Every episode we have recorded for us shows a combination of the two. His courage to speak up about the food they were given when they first arrived in Babylon was born out of a desire not to drift away from observing the dietary requirements of worshipping God. When confronted with Nebuchadnezzar's dream he found courage to speak the truth after seeking God in intimate prayer. When, years later, the time came for the handwriting to be interpreted, Daniel was called upon because he was recognised as having wisdom which came "from the holy gods". Finally, he was called on to have courage in a cavern of carnivores but it came because he had deliberately pursued intimacy with God.

When I was little I went to Sunday school and we sang 'Dare to be a Daniel, dare to stand alone'. It was a great cry to courage but it missed the intimacy. We also sang 'Turn your eyes upon Jesus, look full in His wonderful face', which is a beautiful cry to intimacy but it wasn't linked to courage. We need both together.

As a Christian teacher you will face tough decisions, be presented with difficult moral situations and come under considerable pressure to leave aside your desire to honour the Lord and go the way everyone else is heading. There will rarely be ready-made answers. You will need wisdom and determination to work through them and to fulfil your responsibilities with integrity and peace. The source of your strength and insight will come from the depth of your intimacy with the Lord.

There is nowhere else to go, there are no short cuts, no easy fixes but we cannot bring godly change to our situations or those of the pupils and colleagues we care for without finding wisdom and courage from the depths of our own relationship with God.

What this looks like will vary. Different people will find different methods to suit different lives. What is important is that we explore every possibility until we find what works, because a journey of exploration into God's purpose for you will always be rewarded. 'For everyone who asks, receives. Everyone who seeks, finds. And to everyone who knocks, the door will be opened.' (Matthew 7:8)

To think about – what do courage and intimacy look like for you?

Thanks Mrs Wishart

Not all of your teachers will have been a favourite but I'm certain you will still remember many of them. I can recall every one of my primary school teachers, Mrs Willets, Mr Kelly, Mrs Moore, Mr Bloyce, my first Headmaster and Mrs Wishart (pronounced 'wish-heart'). She had a particular impact in my life. I recall one incident when I was about eight. I became really worried about a new idea called colour factor that was being introduced in maths. It ended up with my mum and dad both coming in to see Mrs Wishart who helped me understand how easy it was and that there was nothing to worry about at all. I think she was the first person outside of my family that truly helped me through a major life issue, which was exactly how colour factor appeared to me at the time.

I learned I could trust other people to help me overcome difficulties. I learned it from my teacher and I remember it to this day. I recall nothing else in particular about Mrs Wishart but that doesn't matter to me. She remains an example of care, concern and compassion. I have no idea how much that one incident has influenced me but I think it has probably been considerable.

Thanks again Mrs Wishart.

If the simplest piece of help offered by one teacher could have such an impact on me, think for a moment about the impact that you have in your pupil's lives each day.

We've already seen how Jesus had a profound influence on a lot of people but as far as we know, some of the encounters were as brief as could be. There were occasions when many were healed (Matthew 4:23-25, 15:30, Luke 6:17-19) but how much time did He spend with each one? Nobody knows. The paralysed man lowered through the roof didn't exactly have a long conversation with Jesus but his life was changed forever (Luke 5:17-25). The woman who crept up behind Him just to touch His robe does not seem to have had many moments with the Saviour of humanity but she was transformed by the experience (Luke 8:43-48). The thief on the adjacent cross to the Lord had a few words with Him but you could hardly describe it as 'quality time' (Luke 23:39-43). Are you getting my point?

How many interactions do you have with your pupils? How many conversations? How many hours do they see you during a week, a month, a year? What do they observe you doing? Talking to a group, helping an individual, organising fun activities, teaching new skills, keeping discipline, dealing with stress and tiredness, interacting with colleagues, all of this and more.

When my wife first developed cancer of the bowel we were told that it was incurable. So we knew what she was facing and we knew for her to live we needed the Lord's direct intervention. We also knew whatever the outcome, we would only allow Jesus to receive honour from the journey and we would refuse to give cancer any room to introduce fear or darkness. Within that desire a question for me was 'How much do I tell my pupils?'

I was form tutor to a group of fifteen and sixteen year olds at the time. Some of them knew people in my church community and so would hear about Ann's situation. I had been cultivating an atmosphere of trust and honesty in the group and I knew that they would look very closely at how I would handle myself in these circumstances. I was also mindful of the fact it was not right for me

61

to overburden these young people or to step outside of my professional responsibility, but at the same time they were a thoughtful, caring bunch and I was aware, on the whole, they quite liked me.

In the end I thought about it in this way: when else might they get the opportunity to see how Jesus can help someone walk a pathway like this? So I told them about Ann and gave them permission to ask me how things were, and I also told them I would give as honest an answer as I felt I could. Did I tell them about all of the struggles, the pain for Ann and its impact on me? No, because they were not my counsellors but when they asked how she was and what stage things were at, I would answer honestly and openly at a level I felt was suitable for them.

After she had died, I determined to go into school and see my class within a few days. The news had been shared publicly and so I wanted them to see I was ok, and that they could talk to me if they wanted. One of the girls said to me, 'Sir, we think you are so strong,' and immediately I knew how to respond. 'I'm not', I said, 'I just know where to find strength.'

Every educator brings influence to their pupils, whether we intend to or not, it is unavoidable. Equally, we are aware of all kinds of other influences in their lives through social media, music, TV, peer groups, parents etc. In many ways as teachers we are just one more voice in a world filled with voices.

But we are a voice which can bring a Heavenly perspective.

Suppose in this context we consider two types of influence on our pupils, unconscious and conscious? Unconscious influence is when people begin to do things that those around them do, even though they are unaware of it. For instance when you notice a child walking like their parent does or using words they have heard them use, whether good or bad.

For instance, my dad was a publican and I grew up in the pub. He had a habit of leaning on the bar or a table with his fists clenched, not out of anger or frustration, it was just a natural habit. After I had met Ann she pointed out that I did the same. I'd never noticed it and I was certain Dad had never said, 'Son, this is the way that I want you to lean on a bar'. I simply did it because of my father's unconscious influence.

On the other hand, conscious influence is when we make a point of wanting to direct the people we are leading in a particular way. To take another childhood example, I remember the moment when I had just allowed a door to close on the lady behind me as my dad and I left a car park. He took that opportunity, gently but firmly, to explain to me why holding doors for people was important and guess what? I still do it. That was over fifty years ago, so I was well and truly influenced.

I think Jesus demonstrates both types of influence in His time with the disciples. There were clearly times when He gave them explicit instructions and expected that they would be followed. For example, '"Don't take any money in your money belts—no gold, silver, or even copper coins. Don't carry a traveller's bag with a change of clothes and sandals or even a walking stick. Don't hesitate to accept hospitality, because those who work deserve to be fed.' (Matthew 10:9-10). Later on they received this instruction, 'Then Jesus asked them, "When I sent you out to preach the Good News and you did not have money, a traveller's bag, or an extra pair of sandals, did you need anything?" "No," they replied. "But now," he said, "take your money and a traveller's bag. And if you don't have a sword, sell your cloak and buy one!"' (Luke 22:35-36).

Two apparently contradictory statements, but given the context of each, they were clear for the circumstances they were going into, this is conscious influence.

I expect though there were many things which those disciples did in a manner that had been modelled by Jesus which we have no record of at all. The way that they spoke to an older or weaker person; how they spent time with them and showed respect for them; the way they conducted themselves as guests at meals or in serving others. We get some glimpses into these things, some hints, but few, if any, definite instructions.

In the same way there isn't a definitive manual describing how a believing Christian teacher should run a class of thirty ten-year-olds, so we have to discover the principles and adapt them to suit our circumstances.

So what are we talking about here? In Christian circles we might be more likely to refer to influence as discipleship, but what is discipleship, what does it look like and should teachers be doing it?

The Cambridge dictionary of English defines a disciple as, 'a person who believes in the ideas and principles of someone famous, e.g. Jesus or Ghandi, and tries to live the way that person does or did'. Among the suggested synonyms my favourites are 'crony', 'henchman' and 'yes-man'. Such a definition indicates to me we need to be careful when we use the word discipleship because there are significant opportunities for misunderstanding, especially in the modern context of teachers and education. Some would see it as suggesting the wrong sort of indoctrination or control, and there are plenty of examples where things have gone badly wrong that add weight to that perspective.

Equally if teachers speak of 'influence' without careful explanation, then even the purest of motives and practice can be viewed with suspicion. Overall then, I believe we should firstly be aware of this principle because it is a significant way the Holy Spirit of God will work through us as teachers. As we give ourselves more and more to His influence in our lives, we should secondly ask for great wisdom, compassion and grace to make sure we do it well. Thirdly, we should pray any influence we do have is all focused towards Jesus so our lives, classes and schools direct pupils towards His life and not away from it.

To think about – how does the Lord desire you to use the conscious and unconscious influence he has given you?

An Atmosphere of Affirmation

West Berlin, 1979. A lone Englishman walks the streets of a foreign city filled with mystery and quite possibly, spies. He has the address of a place to stay but no idea of how to find it, and worse still, no clue whatsoever how to communicate in German except for a few phrases which, although extremely useful in WWII films, he suspects are not going to be very helpful to him right now. What he really needs is someone he knows, which seems unlikely, as he doesn't really know anyone in Germany, let alone Berlin. He prays and his prayer goes something like this: 'Help.'

He turns a corner and walks into two men he had talked to all of the previous night in a German service station where they were trying to hitch-hike from. Seriously, what are the chances?

The lone Englishman was of course me and the two guys were real enough, I didn't imagine them; or at least I don't think I did. They told me which metro train to take and where to go to find my half-brother's flat which was where I was heading. He was a motorbike mechanic who had been there for a few years and who was providing a useful stop-off point for me as I hitched around Europe.

It was one of my earlier experiences of God working in the most extraordinary and unusual way. I needed help, no question at all, but I look back and realise God was enjoying Himself. What I mean to say is, He was watching over me and the bizarre situation I had landed myself in, and He was enjoying showing me that this was ok, it wasn't the mess I thought it was, because He was there with me.

I'll rewind a little. I finished my A-Levels in 1978 but didn't exactly set the world on fire with my results. Somehow I secured a place at university because frankly it wasn't so difficult then, but I was keen to take a year out and do something other than study for a while. Gap years hadn't really been invented then, so this was considered a bit irresponsible at the time. There was a suspicion I was in danger of wasting my time. I thought differently, of course, because I was eighteen and knew everything; enough said.

Looking back, I realise one vital element missing from this whole escapade was some conversation with the Lord. It wasn't because I didn't pray! Of course I did, I was a Christian, went to church and did all of the proper stuff. What I mean is, I wasn't praying about what I was doing, or why I was doing it. I didn't realise it was a part of the deal. I'm sure the people in my church had told me something about it because they were good people and they loved Jesus. It's just the idea of God being really interested in me and what I was doing with my life hadn't properly taken root. I've spent the forty or so years since then trying to get to grips with that idea.

God has purpose for your life and He has purpose for your pupil's lives.

Many of your pupils will have scant, if any, comprehension of the truth of God's love or of His desires for them but we can help by providing a context of confidence in their futures. You won't always have the freedom to explain the reason for your outlook but an atmosphere of affirmation dispels doubt. Your pupils will feel the hope that you have through the Holy Spirit and it will begin to change their perception of themselves. It isn't salvation but it is the kindness of God that can lead them towards salvation (Romans 2:4).

The atmosphere we foster externally is determined by what we have already received internally. What is real to us on the inside will inevitably colour everything we do on the outside.

So how do we receive and grow it on the inside?

'"For I know the plans I have for you," says the Lord. "They are plans for good and not for disaster, to give you a future and a hope."' (Jeremiah 29:11) It's a commonly quoted verse when we consider the future, but have you ever wondered how God can work to a plan when we keep messing it up so much? At quite a tender age I realised I had probably already messed up plans A, B, C, D etc. and I wasn't too sure how many chances I had left.

Another confusing thing when I was younger was a bit more theological. God was the boss, He knew everything and the general idea was to obey Him; no questions, no room for manoeuvre. On the other hand, I was also being told I had this thing called freewill, and so I could do absolutely whatever I wanted, but it was a good idea to check with Him first, so as to make wise choices even though He already knew what I would choose anyhow. This made no sense to me at all. If God knew I would make lousy choices, why allow me to do it in the first place? What was even more aggravating was that all of the older, and supposedly wiser, people I asked for some explanation just nodded their heads sagely and said stuff like, 'Yes, it's a mystery, isn't it?' I already knew it was mysterious, why else was I asking them? Frankly, they weren't much help at all. I then discovered people had been giving the same answers for years and years and years anyway. It seemed to me that nobody was giving any clear answers anywhere.

You're probably thinking I should have asked the Holy Spirit for help, well maybe I should have but we hadn't really been introduced properly at that stage and so I didn't realise it was an option. It was only years later I began to think about things differently. It was then I started to see God's plans are rooted in a much deeper purpose.

Think of it this way, when you want to travel somewhere you may have a specific route in mind but things don't always go as you expect, just like my experience in Berlin. You may have to alter your original journey because of a delay or obstacle, but your goal is still the same. You know where you're going but the way to get there is flexible. I believe God works in a similar way. He has a purpose for each individual which He is completely committed to seeing achieved. We try to cooperate with Him but our imperfections tend to throw up obstacles. He, in His infinite wisdom and love, accommodates for these and so we find His help in our time of need.

Your pupils need to discover the same confidence, which is impossible without knowing God personally, but the amazing thing is, God has placed them in your care. Perhaps you can't speak to them directly about God but the possibilities for God to work through you in their lives are as great as His love for them. We should not underestimate the incredible difference we can make to them because our confidence in the Holy Spirit is shaping the atmosphere of the classroom.

Over thirty years after that time in Berlin I was looking for my half-brother again, this time in an intensive care unit in a London hospital. When I found him I was shocked. There were tubes, machines, screens, bleepers, wires and there he was in the middle of all of them. He didn't look in a good way but people rarely do two days after an aneurysm ruptures at the base of their brain. He wasn't able to respond to me, of course, but I was there to pray and suddenly I wondered if I had the faith and courage to do so.

When it came to faith I found the surroundings more of an obstacle than an encouragement, there was nothing there to help me. I was in an unfamiliar atmosphere and so was not able to find the affirmation I needed from it. All of the resources I needed had to be found somewhere else; they had to be found internally. I'd love to tell you that I prayed aloud and confidently with immediate results being seen as he leapt from the bed but it wasn't like that. I prayed quietly for a couple of minutes then left.

It wasn't until months later as I spoke to him on the phone one day that I was able to see how by the grace of God and with the help of many fine medical professionals, my prayers had been answered. I can identify a similar process in operation with many of my pupils, long after they have left my classroom. I fully acknowledge the help and support they have received from many others but I always give thanks for everything God is doing in their lives, because I know that I have also played a part in it.

To think about – how can you develop a stronger atmosphere of the Holy Spirit's affirmation of your pupils through your own teaching?

Sensitivity

Early in my teaching career I developed a now unshakeable belief, every child who was in front of me in any class was placed there by God. My reasoning was simple, if I was there by divine appointment, then so were they. This might sound as though I was developing an over-inflated ego, not at all. I was simply recognising the incredible desire of God to make disciples that would make more disciples. (2 Timothy 2:2 and Matthew 28:18-20)

This meant that everyone I taught was not only someone who God loved so much that He gave Jesus as a Saviour for them, but also every one of them was a potential younger brother or sister in God's family. This was a challenging thought because they certainly didn't always act in a way which made me think they were aware of the same truth. Some of them could really be quite annoying potential younger brothers or sisters. I expect you know what I mean.

What it did do was begin to open my heart to the possibility the Father might want to communicate something special at any moment. A colleague of mine in a Christian school had the habit of praying for her class before the start of each year and writing a small card out with anything she felt the Lord indicate to her. One year she had a group of eight or nine year olds and was reminded of Isaiah 49:16, 'I have written your name on the palms of my hands.' as she prayed for one girl in particular. She wrote this out on a card with a simple explanation and left it on her desk as she did for all of her class.

What she didn't know was the girl was adopted and at this particular stage of her life she had a deep need to know she was special and cared for individually. The result was not only did that girl come to know Jesus but her parents and their other adopted child did also. It is amazing how God can work in someone's life when we are sensitive to His voice and prompting.

The method employed there may not work in your situation but don't be deterred from being open to the possibilities presented to you.

For many years I taught Religious Studies to fourteen to sixteen year olds with half of the time being devoted to Christian ethics. It was a wonderful opportunity to explore significant issues such as abortion, euthanasia, war, peace, sexuality and so on. On one occasion, whilst explaining about Christian attitudes to abortion, I was using the example of Psalm 139:13-16, 'you knit me together in my mother's womb'. In the class was a young girl of sixteen who was not normally noted for her enthusiasm in matters of academic pursuit but she did show interest in some of the ethical issues. This was such a time.

After I'd finished my particular point I set them off on some related work but this girl put up her hand. 'I don't understand what this has to do with abortion,' she informed me. Clearly my teaching wasn't as good as I thought it was. I invited her to come to the front desk so I could explain further. As I began to do so I was quickly aware of some extra emphasis in the conversation. It wasn't caused by anything she said or did, it was an inner conviction or weight to the moment not previously there which was coming from the Holy Spirit. I knew in some deeper way this was a significant conversation for her and I was to pay attention to what God was doing.

She showed no signs of recognising any moment of divine intervention in her life, and at the end of my, hopefully improved, explanation, she went back to her seat and carried on in her usual manner.

When Jesus fed 5,000 people I think we can be fairly sure for most of them it was not a moment of conversion. In fact I suspect the ones furthest away from Jesus probably though there was just a huge supply of food somewhere out of sight. For those closer in to where Jesus was they may have witnessed more but we are not told. It is quite possible the vast majority of those fed simply got a good meal.

Our classes will not always be significantly changed by what we do and say but this should never discourage us. The more we are sensitive to His voice, the more we will be confident that He is working through us into our pupil's lives.

We cannot imagine Jesus becoming disillusioned by a lack of visible impact. His work was to do what pleased His Father. He didn't play to the crowd nor did he pander to important individuals. His responses were to what His Father was doing and saying, (John 5:19). So when He came across an individual that He knew His Father wished to touch, He responded straight away; a woman at a well (John 4); a blind man by a roadside (Mark 10); a woman in a crowd (Luke 8); a disabled man by a pool (John 5). As He passed each one I'm sure there was communication from the Father which let Him know 'this one needs your attention now'.

The question is, how do we develop a higher level of sensitivity to God's leading in the hurly burly of school life? I have some suggestions.

Pray specifically for the classes and situations you are in, perhaps even as you enter or move towards the room or space. This helps us to focus ourselves and lets the Holy Spirit know we are awake to His work in the moment.

Believe you are there by divine appointment and therefore you are significant in God's plan for that place and those people.

Expect God to be showing you what he is doing. Pray with faith, not in unbelief.

Don't underestimate your capacity to be His representative.

I am convinced when we are operating with sensitivity to the Holy Spirit we can leave the results up to Him.

To think about – how can you further develop your personal sensitivity to the prompting of the Holy Spirit at work in your classroom?

Holiness and Wisdom

I was minding my own business going into a prayer meeting one day. It was nothing in particular to do with education really, just a group of local people involved in church leadership who met regularly at lunchtime to pray for our city. As I strolled casually towards the church building a question popped into my thoughts which had definitely not been there earlier. I asked the Lord, 'What do you really want for education?' Immediately the answer came back in one word, 'Holiness'. I knew it was the Holy Spirit speaking to me because I would never have come back so quickly on my own or with such an unhelpful answer.

When I say 'unhelpful' I probably need to qualify what I mean because I don't want to give the impression that I consider the Holy Spirit unhelpful in any way whatsoever. It was just a bit obscure as far as I was concerned. Partly because I knew that my question related to all education, not only Christian expressions within it and partly because holiness is not really a part of most school curriculum planning.

Clearly I was going to have to think about this a bit more.

I went into the prayer meeting, collected the very fine coffee and biscuits that my good friend the Baptist pastor was providing and sat down to pray. The problem was that I couldn't focus on what everyone else was praying, because I was so intrigued by what the Lord had just said to me. What did He mean?

As I was considering this I began to think about the tabernacle in the desert. The tabernacle was all about holiness, wasn't it, so it seemed like a good place to start. The instruction manual for it was quite exacting, like a divine self-assembly guide. Highly specific details of dimensions, structure and materials fill pages of text, which in many ways you could say was a bit unreasonable. They were in the desert and they were moving around quite a bit and neither of those factors seem conducive to building such an important and ornate structure, even though it was designed as portable.

The purpose of the structure was so God could live among the Israelites (Exodus 25:8). God isn't going to live anywhere that doesn't reflect His holiness, right? So the place had to be built in such a way that it was set apart, holy. The materials were costly and were given sacrificially and in honour of Him, and the plans were intricate and delivered straight from Heaven. We then get to the guy in charge and here is where things start to relate to teaching a bit more.

Bezalel was the man chosen and God said, 'I have filled him with the Spirit of God, giving him great wisdom, ability, and expertise in all kinds of crafts' (Exodus 31:3). He is, as far as I know, the first person mentioned in the Bible who was 'filled with the Spirit of God'. In his case, holiness was a quality given to him through his experience with wisdom. The wisdom He received showed itself in his capacity to carry out the tasks laid out through the revelation given to Moses.

If we fast forward several hundred years to Solomon, we find someone else who was filled with godly wisdom through the application of choices he made through life. Solomon was also to build a place for God to live among His people, as his father David had been prevented by the Lord from doing so himself. Although we are given some description of what the Temple was like, there is little indication these were direct instructions received from the Lord. Could it be Solomon's instructions were simply divinely inspired through the great wisdom he had already asked for and clearly accumulated?

We can see God's response to Solomon's preparations in 1 Chronicles 7:1-3, 'When Solomon finished praying, fire flashed down from heaven and burned up the burnt offerings and sacrifices, and the glorious presence of the Lord filled the Temple. The priests could not enter the Temple of the Lord because the glorious presence of the Lord filled it. When all the people of Israel saw the fire coming down and the glorious presence of the Lord filling the Temple, they fell face down on the ground and worshipped and praised the Lord, saying, "He is good! His faithful love endures forever!"'

Powerful, yes?

It seems to me in both these cases, Moses' tabernacle and Solomon's Temple, the application of wisdom led to an encounter with holiness. I realise that there are all kinds of conditions and caveats that you might think of but let's keep it simple shall we? After all, Jesus said on more than one occasion that we needed to be like small children to fully receive the kingly rule of the Father. Simply put then, wisdom leads to holiness.

Let's consider this for a moment, as teachers who spend our lives trying to impart God's wisdom to our pupils. If God's desire in education is to see holiness as an outcome, it can only happen with His help. After all, He is the only source of holiness. However, if wisdom leads to holiness, the implication is that we are, in some way, cooperating with God to create pathways which could lead our pupils to discover God's holiness for themselves.

As Christians who teach, we are constantly engaged in the pursuit of God's purpose for ourselves, as well as our pupils. If the fruit of this pursuit is holiness, then we are working towards something incredibly wonderful and beautiful.

To think about – what might wisdom which leads to holiness look like in your setting?

Isaiah 35 for Teachers

This chapter and the two others like it are written as devotional pieces, to allow time to reflect on whatever the Lord may be saying to you. Read them differently to the rest of the book. Take a little time and allow the Holy Spirit to engage with you and reveal His truth to you. I have used different versions of the Bible for each one but feel free to use whichever suits you best.

Clearly, this passage was not originally written into our educational context but the heart behind its inspiration is the same heart that we appeal to, and draw life from today. May you find fresh relevance and revelation in it now.

1 The wilderness and dry land will be joyously glad! The desert will blossom like a rose and rejoice!

As you read through this, try to 'hear' it on various levels. Try to see it as applying to an individual pupil, to a class, to a school and to a nation. Don't forget to see it as applying to you as well. Prophetic writing like this is multi-faceted and needs to be understood in that way. How else can a Lord, as great and wonderful as He is, communicate His intentions to us?

² Every dry and barren place will burst forth with abundant blossoms,

> *dancing and spinning with delight!*
> *Lebanon's lush splendour covers it,*
> *the magnificent beauty of Carmel and Sharon.*
> *My people will see the awesome glory of Yahweh,*
> *the beautiful grandeur of our God.*

The images of Carmel and Sharon convey fruitfulness, bounty and pleasant prosperity of every kind. Can you get a vision of the hearts of your pupils dancing and spinning with delight as your example of, and transmission of, the truth through your teaching leads them towards the source of their liberty, healing and destiny? If not then why not ask the Holy Spirit to help you right now, it is truly His desire to do so.

³ Strengthen those who are discouraged.

> *Energise those who feel defeated.*

⁴ Say to the anxious and fearful,

> *"Be strong and never afraid.*
> *Look, here comes your God!*
> *He is breaking through to give you victory!*
> *He comes to avenge your enemies.*
> *With divine retribution he comes to save you!"*

We all feel the need to latch onto the promises of strengthening and energising at times, don't we? At the same time we can be nervous of receiving victory. Somehow it can seem a bit too much for us, but we need to keep in mind whose victory we are sharing in and why. We share in God's triumph because He has placed us in His triumphal procession (2 Corinthians 2:14). Let's not be reticent to receive what he has chosen to give us as our inheritance. Don't we all want to see God right any wrongs and redress the balance in the lives of the individuals in front of us where it needs to be?

5 Then blind eyes will open and deaf ears will hear.
6 Then the lame will leap like playful deer
   and the tongue-tied will sing songs of triumph.
   Gushing water will spring up in the wilderness
   and streams will flow through the desert.

What could this mean to individuals you teach? Where are the difficulties they face? Where are the seemingly impossible circumstances you would love to see them overcome? Can you bring those before the only One who has the capacity to bring change? Could you possibly be a part of His loving and powerful response?

7 The burning sand will become a refreshing oasis,
   the parched ground bubbling springs,
   and the dragon's lair a meadow
   with grass, reeds, and papyrus.

(There is a footnote to the text explaining 'dragon' can also be translated as 'jackal')

Whether it's a figurative dragon's lair or an actual jackal, it's sounding none too hospitable. If you feel any of your situation is like this, then consider how God desires to bring transformation to it. Remember, even though your situation is not the one that the original text was intended for, the same principles of refreshment and restoration move His heart for you today.

8 There will be a highway of holiness called the Sacred Way.
   The impure will not be permitted on this road,
   but it will be accessible to God's people.
   And not even fools will lose their way.

The Highway of Holiness is not an actual, physical location but it does describe a real enough journey; your journey. It is accessible to you but not to anything that would threaten, harm, hinder or waylay you. You can't even get lost. God's passion for His purpose in you is infinitely stronger than anything which opposes you.

9 The lion will not be found there;
   no wild beast will travel on it—
   they will not be found there.
   But the redeemed will find a pathway on it.
10 Yahweh's ransomed ones will return with glee to Zion.
   They will enter with a song of rejoicing
   and be crowned with everlasting joy.
   Ecstatic joy will overwhelm them;
   weariness and grief will disappear! (TPT)

This sums up the impact of God's good news in our hearts, doesn't it? There is a route in journeying through life with God where we can always find an exchange of joy for weariness and grief. This is His promise to you which can be accessed now, irrespective of your past, whatever your current circumstances and however you view your future. Talk to Him now and bear your heart to your Heavenly Father. His promise is sure and His willingness for you to know the depths of His love is certain.

To think about – can you imagine Isaiah's prophetic vision embracing your daily school experience?

What's In a Name?

Ranelagh Grammar School in Bracknell, Berkshire is my alma mater. It was, and as far as I know, still is, a good school. In my time you had to pass an exam to get in and they must have been low on numbers in 1971, because somehow I got a place there. Like all schools it had its drawbacks, one of which was the uniform cap that I had to wear on the journey to and from school. Thankfully I lived out in the sticks with no public transport, in fact no public at all. So the cap-wearing was confined to the journey to and from Dad's car.

One of Ranelagh's other little idiosyncrasies was boys were known by their surnames whilst girls went by their first names. By current standards it would be cause for all kinds of complaint about discrimination and I'd have probably sued them, or at least insisted on a deal to guarantee good grades. I was called 'Coyle' by all of my teachers which was at best impersonal, but on occasion could be made to sound like a declaration of war, which it occasionally was.

One of the great accolades of school life as a boy was to progress to being called by your first name. When you ascended to those dizzy heights it was a day to remember, especially if you were a sportsman and the teacher concerned was 'Norman' the games master. I still remember the time it happened to me.

I was by the lockers which, back in my era, were more like wooden slatted, open boxes. I was minding my own business when 'Norman' asked me a question. I don't remember what he asked me, but I remember who he asked, he asked Graham. I was fifteen and a good year or two ahead of the normal surname to first name transition. It was as unexpected as it was incredible, at least at that stage of my life when such things were disproportionately important. I had arrived, I had a name; I was someone.

Names are an important concept in the Bible because they are more than just a label. They denote identity and purpose. If we know someone's name it is for a good reason. When God announced to Mary she would give birth to Jesus He was showing her incredible favour but she was not allowed to select a name, it was already firmly decided by the Father. As another example I have met many people named after the apostles, Peter, John, Andrew, and even Bartholomew, but never anyone named Judas. The reasons are obvious, aren't they?

Equally we name girls Rebecca or Elizabeth, but not Jezebel. We realise that a name can be so much more than an identifier.

In Revelation 2:17 we read of overcomers being given a name known only to themselves and God. Think about that for a moment in relation to yourself. Don't worry too much about the details, just focus on the idea of an identity you have which is known only to you and God.

'Hang on a minute,' you might be saying, 'I don't know anything about any name, it can't be true.'

Why not though? Just because you don't know it yet, it doesn't mean that God hasn't given it. After all, if He is giving the stone with the name on it, it suggests He has got the name already prepared as well, doesn't it? Not surprising really for the all-knowing One. I don't imagine a vast hopper filled with stones and each one getting given a new name on the basis of a lucky dip. No, this is unique to you. You have a name, you have a purpose.

To me this conveys love, care, dignity, divine selection, destiny. How much better a name than a number? God's people are free people and are overcomers, their names denote this in a specific way. The Father knows us so intimately, He sees every area in our lives where the victory of Jesus will be applied personally.

There are two specific reasons why this is important to us now. You have a name and an identity in God's grace, but consider this, so do your pupils. Wouldn't it be exciting if we were operating with greater insight into these things?

One of the things I did over many years was to pray by name for my pupils. Not with them present, but in their absence before or after school, or when I was at home. Sometimes by walking around the classroom and stopping at their places, sometimes when marking their work. I named them specifically. I wanted to draw the attention of Heaven to them. I didn't reel off a list of the things that I want God to sort out about them. I prayed for their futures, I asked God for wisdom to lead them in the way that He was leading and not simply according to my own perception.

I named them as I imagined myself standing in Heaven, because I didn't know how many other people were doing so and I had the privilege of knowing them personally. I wasn't overestimating my importance in their spiritual life but I certainly didn't want to underestimate it. As a believing teacher I knew I had God's attention for my pupils and he wanted me to cooperate with His purpose for them.

I believe this relates to another experience. For many years my family attended the same Christian family camp. Ann and I had been a part of the ministry that ran it and after we moved on, they kept asking us back to run the camp radio station each year. It was huge fun and we always looked forward to it immensely. Although the radio was an annual highlight, my favourite aspect of the camp was the opportunity to gather with thousands of other Christians to worship.

Yes it was in a huge showground barn, yes it could be drafty and cold, even in August, and yes, the place smelled of sheep but it was truly glorious. I love to get completely lost in 'wonder, love and praise' and the camp meetings were a great opportunity to do so.

On one particular occasion I became aware of an image forming in my imagination. Some might call it a vision, but I don't wish to label it in case I'm misunderstood. Suffice to say that it struck me powerfully.

I imagined myself worshipping before God's throne, as in Revelation 19, but I was surrounded by children and young people. Some of them I knew because I had taught them but many I did not. What did become apparent to me was they were all there in part because of what God had called me to do with my life. The impact of seeing people in that numberless crowd of captivated worshippers, who were helped there through my weak and flawed efforts to faithfully follow Jesus, broke me. In a moment I realised a part of my own identity as a child of the Father was tied up in this image.

It was probably a couple of decades ago but it is as meaningful to me now as ever, because it was God revealing something which I had not previously known about myself or His purpose in my life. The Bible talks of the hidden mysteries of our souls which cannot be known by any other human (1 Corinthians 2:11) but if the mysteries of our hearts are entwined with God's own heart, then we begin to understand who we are and how we are to be in this world. Without the Spirit's guidance in this way, we could live as great servants of the Lord but miss what it is to know Him fully in the same way that friends know each other (John 15:15).

When we pray for our pupils by name we recognise their uniqueness. We are acknowledging that the individuality of each one is precious to the Father. We work alongside a principle in Heaven which He has established. All of these things give a significance to the activity of praying which can become lost if we are not careful.

To think about – why not pray for your pupils and name them in Heaven now?

The Long and Winding Road

Question: what do Fauja Singh, a 92 year old Punjabi-born Sikh man, Paula Radcliffe the famous and extraordinary British athlete and I have in common? Answer: we all ran in the 2003 London Marathon. Yes indeed, I raced against them both, along with 36,000 or so others. I know you are all immediately wondering about the finishing order. Well, let me tell you that Paula had a head start, as the elite women's race began before the less than elite bit I was in, so naturally she crossed the line ahead of me. Without such an advantage, who can say what the outcome might have been? As for Fauja, I'll tell you at the end of the chapter.

The London Marathon was first run in 1981 and I had a hankering to run it then whilst still at PE College. A friend of mine ran it the following year but I didn't get around to it until much, much later. The thing with a marathon is this; it is a long way, a very long way, a long, long, long, long way. To be precise 26.2188 miles or 42.195 kilometres; as I said, a long way. Serious training for me began about eight months in advance and, even though I say so myself, I worked pretty hard to be ready. I spent a lot of time out on country roads near to my school, uphill and down dale, in sun, rain and wind, and a good question is, 'why?' Why did I do it? Well I mostly did it because I thought it would be fun and I also really wanted to finally stop saying, 'I'm going to run a marathon someday'.

Those things kept me going. What keeps you going?

You see, life is a long way as well. You might have heard people say that life is a marathon, not a sprint. They're wrong, it isn't just a marathon. Every year across the globe thousands upon thousands run marathons, many of them just like me, not really runners at all, just people who want to do one. These people prove marathons can be done and then left behind. Great memories, a commemorative medal hanging on a wall, but nothing more. Life isn't like that. There are no practice runs, only the main event and you only get one shot at it. You can't think 'Next time I'll get it right,' as this is it, a glorious, wonderful, exciting once-in-a-lifetime, God-given opportunity.

Thankfully we don't all have to run marathons to appreciate this, we can learn in other ways. We certainly need to as Christian educators. Life isn't a sprint and the academic year isn't a sprint, I'm sure you know this. To successfully negotiate the rigours of the year requires an ability to pace yourself.

Jesus was good at pacing himself, he was never in a hurry. He frequently told people He was only giving His time and attention to the things His Father was doing (John 5:19, 8:28). That's why He always appeared to be in control and never panicked. If He didn't sense it from Heaven, then He didn't allow it into His life. His agenda and timetable were determined by His relationship with the Father.

"Ah yes", I hear you say "But what about school timetables, deadlines, appointments, end of term, Heads of Departments, senior leadership teams and the like? Jesus didn't have those, did he?" No, but are we really saying that Jesus didn't have pressures in life, didn't feel the intensity of the battle He was in? The temptations He faced following His baptism and commissioning were all about His identity as God's Son and His purpose as the Saviour of humanity (Luke 4:1-13). If Jesus was tempted in every way as we are (Hebrews 4:15), doesn't it follow our temptations will test the same qualities in us as they did in Jesus? They will test our identity and our purpose?

Running the London Marathon is an extraordinary experience for many reasons but perhaps mostly because of the crowds. The support and encouragement derived from them is incredible. Literally thousands line the streets and none of them are running. In 2003 it was a warm day and the pubs and cafés en route were doing a great trade in coffee, beer and soft drinks. Many of them had barbecues going, the smells of which were tantalising. Which frankly wasn't fair and should have been outlawed! There was an atmosphere of enjoyment and celebration for the crowds, but temptation and frustration for the thousands of us who could only dream of enjoying such things when we finished.

What was significant though was the fact that everyone in the crowds wanted everyone in the race to do well. It didn't matter who I was, what charity I was running for or how I looked, everywhere I went people got behind me and cheered me on.

The halfway point is on Tower Bridge and when I reached there I was still feeling strong and running a respectable time. We then headed off into Canary Wharf which was fine until somewhere around mile eighteen or so, then it happened; 'the wall'. You may have heard of 'the wall', I certainly had and now I was discovering what it was all about. It isn't a physical wall, but it might as well have been. In the space of about half a mile I went from thinking 'I've got this in the bag' to 'put me in a bag'. Fatigue, pain and the sheer impossibility of what I was attempting were all a part of the wall I had hit. At the same time so were the accusations, 'You should have done this ten years ago', 'You haven't trained enough', 'There is a 92 year old Sikh in front of you somewhere', 'A man dressed in a rhino costume has just passed you', 'Graham, you are just not good enough!'

Support from the crowds was still high, but it wasn't enough. I needed more. Now, I don't want to over-spiritualise this, it was just a long run after all, but I reasoned, God had taken me through everything else, he can take me through this. He hasn't fashioned me to be someone who gives up and so I need to find a legitimate and workable strategy to enable me to continue and complete this.

Everywhere I looked at this point were first aiders and race volunteers who were helping people like me. They were massaging cramps out, dealing with dehydration and giving energy-boosting snacks to people who seemed to be dropping like flies. It wasn't pride but I knew if I stopped for help I would not get going again. So I slowed down and started to do what had earlier on been unthinkable; I started walking.

Sometimes in life we need to walk. Pride needs to be got over, goals need to be adjusted and priorities sorted in order to slow down and walk. We might be highly motivated, beautifully honed and rigorously trained, but when we have given all we can, there comes a point when we say, "Ok, I can't keep this pace up, but I can manage a slower pace."

This can attack our sense of personal achievement big time. It isn't a problem for everyone but it is for most, including me and possibly including you. Christian teachers as a breed, I have discovered from personal experience, are dedicated, caring, enthusiastic, effective and often stubborn. We can adopt a mind-set that views any alteration to our plan as a failure and this can be so unhelpful to us. Too many good servants of God are hitting a 'wall' in teaching and the result can take a heavy toll emotionally, mentally, physical or spiritually.

Not only is it unhelpful, it is a lie. A change of plan is not a failure, it is a change of plan. A change of pace is not a disgrace, it is usually a necessary strategy to enable us to overcome what is in front of us and still pursue our desire.

I walked and ran alternately for the rest of the race. I ran when I could and walked when I needed to, but I kept moving forward. Every now and then I ran further than I thought I could, and what made the difference was the crowd. Everyone needs a crowd. Think about that for a moment (Hebrews 12:1). Your crowd of supporters immediately around you may not be huge, but there is a crowd who are cheering you all of the way and they are led by your chief cheerleader; Jesus. Know who your crowd are, thank them, take strength from the encouragement they offer and don't imagine that you can run this ultra-marathon of life without them.

As I approached Big Ben I had about a mile to go to the finish, all of which I managed to run. I have no idea who shouted for me but I'm grateful they did because it got me over the line. Once there I staggered, limped and hobbled through the various end of race procedures and eventually met up with my family. I haven't run a marathon since, but the lessons I learned have been used almost daily.

As for Fauja Singh, the 92 year old Sikh, I ran up behind him somewhere in the vicinity of St Paul's Cathedral and left him in my wake. The next time I saw him was on the TV coverage which strangely didn't include me.

To think about – are you good at allowing God to help you pace yourself? Who is in your crowd?

Light and Darkness

When I was a teenager I was, in common with all other teenage boys, indestructible. I had been a big fan of Marvel comics in my earlier years and learned something important from them: I was a hero, I probably had superpowers and I was certainly more than a match for anything which came my way. This, of course, was frequently put to the test and it proved to be true again and again. I grew up as an only child in the country surrounded by trees, rivers, abandoned buildings and the like, all of which gave me ample opportunity to hone my superpowers and practice saving the world.

My fairly small and quite conservative country village church were unaware of all this and frankly they were a bit slow to recognise just who they had among them. It was ok though, I forgave them because superheroes are supposed to have alter egos, aren't they? I was a part of their youth group, which in itself was an interesting set up because, for most of my years between thirteen and eighteen, there were just three of us who could be described as youth. We were a small but select bunch.

Let me go off at a tangent here, simply to acknowledge two guys who at different times led this group: Derek Warner and Colin Fowler. They did not pretend to be heroes, they did not possess superpowers, they did not even suspect themselves to be leaders, I imagine, but they played highly significant roles in my teenage years and I don't think I'd have survived church life without them.

Tangent exhausted for the moment. I was around sixteen and we were on a church day out near a beauty spot called Symonds Yat. If you don't know it, look it up. It is a beautiful area on the River Wye flowing through a deep, limestone valley. We were on a path high up on one side and came across some caves. For some reason I was on my own at this point, and so decided, like any self-respecting superhero, to enter one of them.

It was pitch black, I had no torch, no helmet or safety gear, no mobile phone of course, as it was the mid-1970s, and most significantly, no idea of what was in the cave beyond the first few steps. But hey, I was indestructible, what could possibly go wrong?

I was also preternaturally wise, so advanced into the cave carefully, slowly and with my hand extended at head height to avoid any unseen obstacle; smart, eh? The first ten feet went completely according to plan, such plan as there was. Soon though the situation went a bit pear-shaped. As it turned out unseen physical hazards weren't the issue, it was more the lack of anything physical at all which suddenly became the problem.

In a moment I went from cautious cave-enterer to frantic free-faller. The cave floor disappeared, completely and instantaneously. One second I was ok, the next I was falling in the pitch black darkness. I was alone, in the dark, with no idea what was going to happen next.

One of the functions of schools is to provide protection. I'm sure we would all agree we want schools to be safe places for children to flourish at every age. Although we will all be aware of the increased regulation surrounding the looking after of children in our care, which regrettably, has become more necessary in recent years, I'm not really talking about those things. I'm talking about the atmosphere and culture which develops in schools and classes when fears are not recognised and dealt with.

I'll explain. I recently heard a story from a friend, now an excellent teacher, who excelled at school but still hated it because of the pressure she felt to maintain her success. Her experience of school became warped and so she did not thrive. The impact of this carried through into adulthood and proved to be something very unhelpful for her. Looking back she realises fear of not receiving the rewards of success was stealing the joy which was rightfully hers.

We would all love children to be protected from the pressures which give rise to fear. Sadly, though, we live in a world with many cracks and broken bits in it and there are many things which bring damage to those we teach. Generally we deal with these issues by attempting to keep the darkness at bay. This is the reason we have increased regulation and safeguards and all manner of strategies for intervention and help. All of these are good and necessary but there is another strategy which I feel we lose sight of. What if the atmosphere that was generated in our classes and schools was so filled with God's light that the darkness just couldn't get a look in? (Isaiah 9:2)

The metaphor of darkness is powerful. When a room is dark, we can switch on a light. The light fills the room, the darkness goes, that's the way it works. We don't get random areas of darkness resisting the light and refusing to budge. It's a physical impossibility.

When it's dark we can see nothing, and if we are in an unfamiliar setting, then we feel uncertain and insecure. As soon as there is light, we can see what's around us and we have a chance to navigate it. Education is filled with potential pitfalls. Teachers who walk and live in God's light carry hope to their pupils to steer a course around the dangers and pitfalls they can encounter.

The cave I was in was dark and my superpowers were letting me down. I was falling and I didn't know how far. You may have heard it said, 'Your life flashes before your eyes'. Mine didn't. To be honest

I can't remember exactly what did flash before them, but what surprised me most was just how many things could tumble through my mind in the half second or so it took me to tumble to the bottom of what might have been a bottomless pit.

Half a second, that was it. Not a very impressive fall really. I landed on my knees on smooth clay, stood up, turned around and looked back out of the cave to the daylight outside. I had fallen no more than four feet and from my new vantage point I could see everything clearly: the entrance, the lack of things to hit my head on and the lack of floor which caused my downfall, literally. Hindsight is indeed a wonderful thing.

I clambered out and pretended nothing had happened. My indestructible nature was still without question, but I wasn't too sure about my super-senses, because as I left the cave I saw a faintly painted, mostly eroded message in quite small letters at the entrance. Some kind soul was warning people not to enter due to the danger of a fall. 'Thanks a lot!'

Light makes all the difference. Jesus said to us, He is the light of the world (John 8:12) but He also told us to let our light shine (Matthew 5:14-16). The light within us is nothing less than the pure light of Heaven, which shines so clearly and brightly there is no need for a sun or moon in the picture painted for us in Revelation 21.

Light in my cave would have kept me from falling. Light for my teacher friend might have enabled her to be both an academically successful student, and to have thrived to the point where she enjoyed her school experience. Light for our pupils could mean us exposing the lie that they are valued by their achievements, or that their future well-being depends on every grade and report they receive. It might also mean they feel happy and safe in the class environment, because the light of God in us helps us to see and dispel the darkness caused by the fears and insecurities of their peers.

I wish I could say I'd done brilliantly in this area. I suspect not if I'm honest. I tried hard and truly desired to help my pupils to see all kinds of things clearly, but at times I know my own inability to discern light myself meant I didn't always serve my pupils as I would like to have done. I have got better at it though. Sometimes this meant I needed to deal with areas that were not well-lit in my own life, and sometimes I know it was the Father helping me, simply because I kept asking Him to. Overall though, I believe I have progressed in this journey and so will you. Oh, and these days, if I enter an unlit cave, I take a torch. That's called learning.

To think about – where are the poorly lit areas in your own life? Ask the Father to help you see more clearly.

Isaiah 53 for Teachers

This chapter and the two others like it are written as devotional pieces, to allow time to reflect on whatever the Lord may be saying to you. Read them differently to the rest of the book. Take a little time and allow the Holy Spirit to engage with you and reveal His truth to you. I have used different versions of the Bible for each one but feel free to use whichever suits you best.

1 Who has believed our report?
And to whom has the arm of the Lord been revealed?

The knowledge of Jesus and the way of salvation are in you because God revealed these truths to you. They didn't happen through chance, your own ingenuity or by mistake. It was all a part of His careful and loving purpose for your life. Why not thank Him for this and ask Him what else He has in His purpose for you?

2 For He shall grow up before Him as a tender plant,
And as a root out of dry ground.
He has no form or comeliness;
And when we see Him,
There is *no beauty that we should desire Him.*
3 He is despised and rejected by men,

A Man of sorrows and acquainted with grief.
And we hid, as it were, our *faces from Him;*
He was despised, and we did not esteem Him.

This brings to mind many children in our schools. They may have no distinguishing beauty, no outward splendour to catch our attention, they may even be despised and rejected by their peers, but doesn't our knowledge of how Jesus was regarded provide us with the insight and compassion we need to help them know that they are loved and respected? Does this bring any particular individuals into your mind?

4 Surely He has borne our griefs
And carried our sorrows;
Yet we esteemed Him stricken,
Smitten by God, and afflicted.
5 But He was *wounded for our transgressions,*
He was bruised for our iniquities;
The chastisement for our peace was *upon Him,*
And by His stripes we are healed.
6 All we like sheep have gone astray;
We have turned, every one, to his own way;
And the Lord has laid on Him the iniquity of us all.

Punishment can be a big deal in our world can't it? I'm not suggesting we disregard the issue of the consequences of selfishness and disobedience in our schools but I do believe we need to rethink our own internal responses. How has God dealt with your rebellion? Did it help you to find Him and to love Him? How can you deal with the rebellion of others in such a way it will point them more towards a loving Father? (Romans 2:4) Do we respond from self-righteousness or from His righteousness?

7 He was oppressed and He was afflicted,
Yet He opened not His mouth;
He was led as a lamb to the slaughter,
And as a sheep before its shearers is silent,
So He opened not His mouth.
8 He was taken from prison and from judgment,
And who will declare His generation?
For He was cut off from the land of the living;
For the transgressions of My people He was stricken.
9 And they made His grave with the wicked—
But with the rich at His death,
Because He had done no violence,
Nor was any *deceit in His mouth.*

We can be misunderstood and treated unfairly. Whatever the reason for a response towards us, we have to keep our own hearts clear of the desire to seek justice in the wrong way and for the wrong reasons. Jesus kept His heart full of love towards His accusers because He always made the choice to focus on what His Father was doing and not what those around Him were doing. Check your own heart now. Is there something getting in the way of you knowing the Father's love for you right now? (Hebrews 3:12-14)

10 Yet it pleased the Lord to bruise Him;
He has put Him *to grief.*
When You make His soul an offering for sin,

He shall see His seed, He shall prolong His days,
And the pleasure of the Lord shall prosper in His hand.

We are now 'in Christ', included in His body the church and so can, by grace, consider ourselves to be caught up in accomplishing the Lord's deepest desires. This is always true for you in each task which is assigned to you. Many of these tasks may appear trivial, burdensome or simply plain, hard slog, but in everything give thanks and search for God's perspective and ask for a way to see joy and peace from the Holy Spirit released to you. Never lose sight of the fact that you are a daughter or son of your Heavenly Father called to accomplish a great purpose. Let His joy be your strength.

11 He shall see the labour of His soul, and be satisfied.
By His knowledge My righteous Servant shall justify many,
For He shall bear their iniquities.
12 Therefore I will divide Him a portion with the great,
And He shall divide the spoil with the strong,
Because He poured out His soul unto death,
And He was numbered with the transgressors,
And He bore the sin of many,
And made intercession for the transgressors. (NKJV)

Not everything good from God is reserved for the future alone. Anticipate His goodness in your current circumstances. Isn't the great paradox of God we can find His perfect will in the middle of imperfect situations? Isn't this the whole message of the gospel? God comes down from the perfection of Heaven to the imperfection of the Earth to bring us back into a loving relationship with Him. This is our source of hope and we can carry it with us everywhere we go.

To think about – what imperfect situations do you need to find the perfect will of God within?

George and the Lion

To say my wife Ann was enthusiastic about animals is an understatement equivalent to describing the Grand Canyon as a large ditch, or the Sahara as a bit sandy. She loved anything that walked, crawled, slithered, flew, swam or in any other way could be described as locomotory. The one exception was those big house spiders, you know, the ones that come in from the cold around the beginning of autumn. She couldn't cope with them at all. She was happy enough that God made them but she just wasn't too sure why He had to make them so they would come into her house. Apart from those beasties everything else was fine.

One of her greatest ambitions was to go on safari in Africa, and one year we had the opportunity. A close friend was working in a children's centre in Uganda and we went to visit her. During that visit we were treated to a three-night stay on a game reserve near to the Murchison Falls on the Nile. Ann was over the moon and we spent almost every moment there watching the most incredible array of African wildlife. For the two of us it was a wonderful and special experience.

People often talk about God giving us the desires of our hearts in a way which makes it sound as though it only works when our desires are linked to what we consider to be high-minded and incredibly spiritual, as if God is only concerned with things of that nature. I know we are encouraged to 'set our minds on things above and not earthly things' (Colossians 3:2) but isn't this to do with the priorities we assign to them? If we were never meant to consider our earthly lives as important we would never wash, eat, change our clothes, go to the doctor, care about the environment or watch sport.

Christians have tried asceticism over the centuries but it has never been a popular option. I believe God placed us on this planet to enjoy it, fill it and look after it well. I believe He wishes us to 'live life in all its fullness' (John 10:10, my paraphrase) and so the best way to accomplish His desire is to get a right sense of priorities. If this were not true I wonder why God would put us in a world like this one in the first place. I don't know how much Ann had prayed about going on safari but I do know it was a gift her Father gave to her and she enjoyed every moment of it.

Much of our time was spent in a suitably battered Land Rover which, although more than a match for the dirt roads and tracks of the reserve, could not by any stretch of the imagination be described as comfortable.

We were out in the park one day, four of us together with our guide, George. George was a local guy who had lived near the park all his life and worked in it since he was old enough to carry a machete. In general terms the age of introduction to using one of these seemed be around five, and believe me, to the uninitiated, it appeared a health and safety nightmare. Just imagine the risk assessment and the paperwork. George was now in his fifties, so he knew his way around the park and was quite used to whatever he found there, including tourists.

Ann wanted to see everything, of course, but in particular she wanted to see lions, who wouldn't? So George took us around to the places where he knew we were likely to find some. This turned out to be easier said than done as the entire lion population seemed to be on holiday. As we bumped and juddered along the tracks, the seats were getting more uncomfortable and the inside of the vehicle was getting hotter, and was developing its own special kind of smell.

'Let's go up onto the roof for a better view,' George suggested. It was the answer to my unspoken prayer so I readily agreed.

Now, as I have already described, the inside of the Land Rover was not built primarily for comfort but at least it had some of the basics, such as seats. The outside of the Land Rover, in particular the roof, didn't even have comfort in the top one hundred considerations. The only concession was the roof bars that at least gave something to hold onto when required, which was basically anytime we were moving and some of the time that we weren't. However, despite the disadvantage of numbness in various parts of my anatomy, I felt an excitement at being in the freedom of the open air as we continued on our lion hunt.

We rounded a few more bushes and then bingo, there they were. A magnificent pair of lions resting in the shade of a tree perhaps fifty yards away. George instructed the driver to slow down but to keep approaching. The lions weren't that bothered about us, which was reassuring. They seemed quite at ease just resting and being the focus of our attention. Everything was going well until a loud, high-pitched, whining sound started in the engine. This was alarming for everyone, most notably the lions who really perked up and started to pay much more attention to their visitors.

Our driver tried to stop the noise but couldn't, as she wasn't too sure what was causing it. She began to back away slowly. I gripped onto the roof bars more tightly, not because it made any difference but because it made me feel better. The lions were no more than thirty feet away, which in terms of, "How far am I from that lion?" is not very far at all. Their demeanour had also changed which gave me the impression I was now observing two very powerful carnivores who were eyeing up the difference between canned meat in the vehicle and fresh meat on the roof.

I invite you to place yourself in my shoes for a moment. I was sitting out in the open on top of a vehicle within a couple of pounces of two of God's beautiful and very effective predators. I began to recall pictures I had seen of safari guides carrying hunting rifles but noticed my trusted Ugandan guide was armed with nothing more than a pair of binoculars. What was he thinking? Was he intending to batter them over the head? I felt unsafe, exposed and uncertain of what was going to happen next.

Then I noticed something else which proved to be terribly important. George wasn't very bothered, in fact he looked quite calm. How was it possible? Didn't he appreciate we were in imminent danger of rapidly slipping down the food chain?

Clearly he didn't, and then I realised why. He had lived and worked around these majestic creatures all of his life, and the truth was that he knew exactly what was going on. He knew what to look for and how to read the signs. So I made a decision, I was no longer going to give my undivided attention to watching the lions, I was now giving rapt attention to George. If he wasn't worried, I wasn't worried. In particular I watched George's eyes. Everything could be seen there and what I saw was peace, and peace was what I needed.

Boom! Then the real truth hit me, it was just like following the Lord. You see I'm safe from everything when I'm with Him. As long as I stick close by Him, and I mean close, then I need fear nothing else because He knows exactly what is going on all of the time. This is His promise to me, and it's His promise to you.

How conscious are we of keeping our gaze fixed on the Lord at all times? Many things clamour for our attention in a day; demands from timetables; the disruptive behaviour of pupils; the extra work caused by things going wrong. All of these and more need to be dealt with, but where is our affection centred? If it is not on the Lord it will be somewhere else.

This can be really hard to achieve in reality, and an example from a safari may seem a bit extreme, but it truly can be applied to our own daily lives.

It comes back to priorities, doesn't it? If our gaze is on Him, if God is our focus, it is difficult to adopt any priorities other than His. When we catch sight of the face of the One who loves us with such intensity, it enables us to stay on track in the middle of the maelstrom.

Teaching in any setting brings us face to face with the priorities others have. However, the priorities of others don't have the authority to shape us, nor do they have the power to tell us what attitudes to adopt or operate with. The way we do our jobs is not dependent on our job descriptions or the demands that go with them. It is dependent on the focus of our affections. Look closely at the One who loves you and follow His lead as you respond to what is presented to you.

To think about – where are your affections focussed in demanding circumstances?

Waves

(To be honest, this particular section isn't specifically about education, but I liked it and so hoped you might as well.)

I woke at 4am. I knew I would because it was really midday, at least it was as far as my body clock was concerned. I had done my best the previous evening to convince myself otherwise but to no avail. I was wide awake and ready for the day. Unfortunately nobody else was.

I had arrived in San Francisco at around 6pm the previous evening and I had processed through US immigration, collected my hire car and made it to the hotel in a couple of hours, which was all pretty pleasing. I had stayed in Half Moon Bay once before, and what was especially attractive about the small hotel was my room was around fifty yards from the beach.

So when I awoke the first thing I was aware of was the sound of the waves rolling along the Pacific shoreline. I was deeply aware of how privileged I was to be there but I was also very conscious of the Lord drawing my attention to the waves. I did the only sensible thing to do at such a time in the morning, I made a cup of tea and got out my laptop to investigate waves in the Bible.

There are around thirty references in the Old Testament to waves, depending on which version you use, and they are almost all bad news. Waves mean peril and disruption, the uncontrollable and unpredictable nature of storms, wind and tempest over the deep, dark seas. Waves can also refer to hordes of soldiers tramping across the deserts or some other terrain, usually bringing death and destruction with them, frequently to God's people as a result of their rebellion, disobedience or just plain old indifference.

It's not a universally true picture, but in large measure as far as God's people were concerned, waves were the harbingers of doom rather than joy.

In the gospels Jesus arrives and paints a very different picture. There are two wavy stories and in both of them Jesus shows He is completely in charge of the waves and that His followers do not have to fear them at all. Firstly we read about Jesus calming the waves and the storm, as in Matt 8:23-27, and then the next time we encounter the dread and terror of the deep, Jesus is walking quite calmly on top of it, Matt 14:22-32.

Clearly Jesus is communicating this, stick close to Him and we will have a capacity for peace and authority in the presence of trouble that will astound us and others.

To think about – when there are waves and storms, how do you make sure you are walking through them with Jesus?

Climate Change

The morning after my wife died I sat on the edge of my all too empty bed and asked God a question: "What do I do now?" I wasn't talking about the immediate now, like what should I do that day? There were plenty of things to do and I had people around me to help, so that wasn't so much the problem. The problem was longer term; what was I going to do with the rest of my life?

I was 53 and it was just few months short of what would have been our thirtieth wedding anniversary. We were both very involved with the work of our church and a large part of my life had been devoted to education and helping young people to work out what they were going to do with their futures. Up until that point I had a fairly clear idea of the future we imagined God was leading us towards, but in asking that question I realised everything had changed.

Up until the previous day the future I had imagined included Ann. There wasn't anything I was involved in which didn't bear the imprint of her love, wisdom and, often, forensic scrutiny in some way. So my question was one of lostness really. I was feeling lost and I wasn't sure what to do about it.

In the moment I asked, an answer came to me.

It's strange how we hear the Lord speak to us sometimes, isn't it? I didn't hear an audible voice, I never have, but I knew His voice as certainly as I had known Ann's.

'Just carry on with what you're doing.'

My personal experience of God speaking is that He doesn't need many words to say a great deal, and in those few words there was a wealth of meaning.

As much as anything else, it was the tone of His voice. Tone reveals so much to us, doesn't it? If someone says our name we can tell immediately what is being communicated to us. Ann, for instance, had many ways of saying 'Graham', admittedly not all in a way I wanted to hear, but I came to learn what most of them meant over the years of our marriage. It is the same with the Lord, we need to learn to discern how He says something, as well as what He says.

In this instance His tone was gentle and compassionate and carried a strong sense of loving affirmation. Although everything had changed for me, nothing had changed about Him. What He had spoken and directed me in previously was still true now and would continue to be so.

This was incredibly important to me because I needed His direction as I'd never needed it before. I also needed to know that the spring of His life within me was still fresh and was still flowing from my intimacy with Him. I'd lost my wife but not my source of life.

How is this experience related to helping your pupils find direction through your work?

I had taught in the same school for almost thirty years and one of the things I love about my length of service there is seeing the direction people find when they move on. Social media has enhanced this capacity to remain in touch and I'm constantly amazed by individuals who do not want to completely dissociate themselves from their former teachers, so stay in touch with me.

I'm not mentioning any names but I am continually thrilled by the quality of lives so many of them live as parents, employees, employers, carers, performers, entrepreneurs, designers and so on.

I ask myself how they found direction and how, if at all, I might have helped.

I am writing this in a café and I have just had a conversation with a lady whose three children I taught some years ago. Two are now married and the third is living at home still and making a successful career as a musician. I heard some of his music played on our local radio station about a year ago; it was really good. I recall a conversation with his dad when he was first contemplating dropping out of college to pursue his dream. Was it a good idea or wasn't it? We didn't know but the evidence is pointing towards him making a good decision.

It serves to illustrate what I'm thinking about. How, as teachers, can we bring good influence that communicates the desires God has in his heart for our pupils? I'm going to describe it as creating a climate of hope.

The café is in a garden centre, which might immediately reveal more about me than I care to admit. Right in front of my table is a big, green, ferny plant. I don't know its name but it is definitely not native to England. Despite this fact such plants are now a common feature for us because we have learned how to create the climate in which they grow and flourish.

For people to grow and flourish they also need a healthy climate, a climate of hope. Ideally schools can provide these climates of hope and teachers are crucial in this. You are crucial to a climate of hope in your school.

Building a climate of hope requires a number of factors. Firstly, we, the teachers, have to cultivate and look after our own hopeful climates. Whatever we have is infectious, so let's make sure we infect people with something good. We can only have genuine hope if we get it from the source of all hope (Romans 15:13). You may be the only person in your classroom who is actively drawing from the

Lord's hope, but be assured, God has chosen you to be there with those individuals and so He will not let your supply run out. The widow helped by Elijah had enough oil for every pot she brought. The implication is the supply would have continued had she found more pots (1 Kings 17:7-16).

A second factor is our discernment. What do we see and what do we hear? I'm not just talking of the more obvious factors here, such as how an individual is picking up a particular skill or not, though such observations coming through the eye of experience are valuable. No, I'm talking about what we see when we ask the Lord about our pupils and He shows us things about them which are only perceived with His help.

A former student came to talk with me once about a choice he was facing between a degree course in a more traditional discipline and one which was designed to lead him into an area of youth ministry. I didn't tell him which to choose, it was his choice to make and he was perfectly capable of making it. I was only being asked for my opinion but I know the bias of my opinion was towards the more traditional degree, as I felt it was a route for him to have influence in two important areas and he could decide later if he wished to focus on one. He decided to ignore my advice and follow what he sensed the Lord saying. I'm so pleased he did, as from what I have observed in the decade or so since then, I think he chose well. As I reflect on the incident I realise I didn't ask the Lord for insight, I simply operated from my natural perception of the abilities and calling of God, and therefore from a personal bias. I was not seeing as God saw and not asking for His help to be able to do so.

What was important in this case is that I should have sensed God had already been speaking to him. My experience leads me to believe this is often the situation young people are in and what they truly need is courage and confidence to follow the direction they are feeling led to. From all that I have said earlier it won't be a surprise to you that I believe this can often be from the Lord. My firm conviction is that young people who do not know God can still be guided by His voice, even when they don't know who is speaking.

What are you saying, Graham? Can young people who have no real relationship with God hear Him and be guided by His voice? Well, yes, I suppose I am. After all, it seemed to work in Samuel's case (1 Samuel 3:7). The way I see it is this. Samuel was a much prayed-for child and he was in an environment of worship and reverence under Eli's authority. Now Eli was far from perfect, as we know, but at least he recognised when God was working in a situation; at least he did eventually. As we know, God can work through any situation He chooses to, so how much more might He be attracted to situations which we invite Him into? Consider again why you are placed in your class or school. To me it seems like evidence God is interested in what happens there and you are his choice to be an effective and faithful witness.

Try it and see what happens, ask the Lord to help you see as He does and then ask for wisdom about how to communicate it.

A third factor to mention is this, a climate looks and feels like something. What do your classes feel like? I was running a series of activities once for groups of teenagers from our school. The purpose of these was to involve them in serving others and going above and beyond what they believed their normal capacities to be. In particular I wanted to see them all growing in their capacity to give and receive encouragement but this was not easy as they lacked the confidence, and skills, to do it well.

I hit upon an idea and to be honest I can't remember where it came from. My suspicion is I borrowed it from someone else so I'm not going to pretend it was originally my inspiration, but it worked well all the same. I got some large, poster-sized sheets of paper along with a good supply of post-it notes and some marker pens. I marked a large grid on the sheets of paper and wrote the name of each person, including staff members, in their own space. I then stuck them up on a wall and left the pens and post-it notes nearby.

Next I encouraged each person to watch what happened during the week and to write down their positive comments on a post-it note, and to stick it in the box to encourage the person concerned. The exercise could be done simply, anonymously and nobody was made to do it but all were encouraged to. I started the process off myself by writing something about everyone so they could see what I meant. Everyone took to the idea and it went so much better than I had hoped for. Within a couple of days there were post it notes everywhere, and the impact of the comments was bringing change to the group.

What I realised was that we were creating a climate of hope, we were changing the culture. It was a simple exercise but it resulted in personal growth for the givers and the receivers, and paved the way for many important principles of God's Kingdom to be demonstrated and understood.

When we cultivate a climate of hopefulness we begin to change the way our pupils perceive themselves and their futures. We help connect them to God's hopeful purpose for their lives, and we begin to see them becoming more open to a relationship with Him in a real way.

My example came from an activity away from school and the group were not all from one class. On our return I began to introduce some of the elements into my classroom practice with good success. So think about your classroom climate and ask God for the strategies which will work for you.

To think about – do you want to bring change to the climate of your classroom? How can you achieve this change and what will it look like?

Staircase

I have led many school trips and on one of those trips we had a wonderful example of what can grow in a climate dominated by God's hope. It came about because teenage boys have a switch in their head that only seems to kick in when they get older. Before that point it allows them to believe they can do things their older, wiser and battle-scarred selves would tell them not to, and they do so without any fear of the consequences. Unfortunately, such belief can at times be misplaced.

The teenage boy concerned felt the best way to escape from his friend chasing him was to jump down half a flight of concrete stairs. It wouldn't have been such a big problem had he not landed awkwardly and broken a bone in his foot. Someone came to break the news to me, which, as you might imagine, was not the best news to receive when leading a group of pupils on a trip in another country.

Inevitably it raised a lot of questions, all of which would need to be worked through, including a visit to a foreign hospital and negotiating the flight and journey home. As a teacher you prepare for these events but never actually expect them to happen. This time it did.

Of course it also created an opportunity to see the Lord at work. This possibility occurred to me straight away, and I was hopeful my pupils would see God do something brilliant.

It was quite late in the evening and having done all of the necessary first aid the decision was taken to head for hospital in the morning, when we could easily take someone local who knew the system and language. What we could do more immediately was pray. How much better if we saw him healed before the hospital visit.

My school was one where prayer with pupils was permitted, the boy was from a Christian family and some in the group had their own faith, but many were unconvinced. I asked the boy's permission and he agreed that he would like us to pray. Gathering the group round, I explained what we were going to do and also told them the story of the ski trip from a few years earlier. Stories of what God has done previously help provide the opportunity for Him to do the same again. I was very confident of us seeing a wonderful healing.

I prayed, other staff prayed and a few of the kids added their own brief prayers. Despite all of this, nothing changed. The bone remained broken and the lad was still in pain. We prayed again and still no change. I can't remember if we prayed a third time or not, but the headline news was, no change.

Learning how to handle these situations is not normally a part of teacher training, is it? It's not even a part of any training course run by Christians for teachers, as far as I'm aware. What's more, the New Testament, and especially Jesus, are unhelpfully silent on what to do when you pray and nothing happens. I've come to the conclusion this is because Jesus didn't want to prepare His disciples for a situation they shouldn't expect to occur.

'"Keep on asking, and you will receive what you ask for. Keep on seeking, and you will find. Keep on knocking, and the door will be opened to you. For everyone who asks, receives. Everyone who seeks, finds. And to everyone who knocks, the door will be opened. You parents—if your children ask for a loaf of bread, do you give them a stone instead? Or if they ask for a fish, do you give them a snake? Of course not! So if you sinful people know how to give good gifts to your children, how much more will your Heavenly Father give good gifts to those who ask Him? (Matthew 7:7-11)

I don't think Jesus prepared us to deal with prayers God wasn't answering because it wasn't in His expectation, and He ought to have known because He was the incarnation of God, wasn't He? Which is fine in theory but here I was with a group of young, somewhat sceptical young people, whom I was confidently telling to expect God to heal their friend, and they were not seeing it happen.

The next day dawned and our young invalid was piggy-backed around the place until we could get him some transport to the hospital. Our hosts in Bulgaria were a Christian school which was filled with pupils who were all feeling very sorry for the patient, and he was getting plenty of sympathetic attention, especially from the girls. I did secretly wonder if this was more attractive to him than getting healed, but kept my thoughts to myself.

I decided to get all of their pupils to pray for him along with ours, because more people praying equals more effectiveness, right? Not necessarily, at least in visible terms, because there was still no change, and so he went off to be attended to in the local hospital.

Meanwhile I had a number of conflicting emotions going on inside myself. I really wanted to see him healed because I felt compassion for him. I couldn't find it in my heart to blame him for having an accident just because he was playing around. Furthermore my experience told me God could, and would, heal him if we asked. On the other hand I wanted the whole group to see God at work in extraordinary ways to encourage them He was real, and could be known and trusted, but it wasn't happening. How was I going to handle this internally and what would the consequences be externally? I'd taken a bold stance of faith and it looked as though the pupils would see, yet again, that there was no action to show God was as good as I said He was.

We went through the next day and a half with not much happening. As far as the boy was concerned the die was cast, and so was the flight-friendly cast around the leg. As far as the boy and his fellow pupils were concerned God hadn't come through, but as He so rarely seemed to, it was no big surprise. We had a day of sight-seeing around Sofia with lifts being provided for our invalid between the places of interest. The evening came, and with it a report from some of the female staff about an 'atmosphere'. You know the kind of thing I mean, the kind of 'atmosphere' I was completely oblivious to, which had arisen between some of the girls. Someone thought someone else had said something, and had therefore said something else back to the first someone. The result was, an 'atmosphere' had developed.

These kind of things are all part and parcel of teaching teens and not so unusual, but on this occasion I knew we needed to deal with it slightly differently. There was something important at stake here, and I wanted everyone to understand what it was and have the opportunity to put it right.

I called everyone together again and explained that we were experiencing a robbery. I invited everyone to think back over the great time they had enjoyed through the week, how they had overcome fears, done things they didn't believe they could do and found they had enjoyed getting on with people they wouldn't normally be close to. I then drew attention to the atmosphere which almost everyone else had been aware of, and showed them how, through misunderstandings and false assumptions, they came to believe lies about each other and themselves. This was giving the enemy of God's goodness the opportunity he needed to divert them from God's blessing. They all paid very close attention, which was as much a sign of God's Spirit at work as I needed.

I then explained what we were going to do about it. In the place where we were staying was a large, open area which formed a focus for everyone gathering together. It was also a warm, dry evening. I told them some of them needed to say sorry to each other for what they had said and done, but in order to help them do this, we were all going to go outside and walk around having conversations with anyone we wished to. Nobody would know what was being said, or to whom, but I was quite clear it was the opportunity to put things right so they should make the most of it.

Amazingly, everyone went outside very obediently and without complaint, nobody went off in a strop and nobody sat in a corner sulking. After around fifteen minutes of people wandering around and chatting, I realised that all of the kids were together by a bench. I went over to see what was happening and saw they were all praying for the lad with the broken foot. It wasn't just gentle prayer, these young people were really going for it, led by one especially bold and faith-filled girl. I decided to keep right out of it and just watch what happened. At one point the girl leading them said 'And we all agree with you, God, that he is healed now in Jesus' name'. It was great praying I thought, but nobody responded to her, so I chipped in and asked, 'Well, do you agree?'

There were a few murmurings and a few of them began to say 'Yeah, I suppose so'. At that moment I knew for certain he was healed. I had no physical evidence yet, but I knew as surely as I knew anything, the healing was complete. The lad confirmed quite quickly that he was no longer experiencing any pain and went off to play basketball with his mates.

On his return home, the hospital did another X-ray and confirmed that the only injury they could find was a minor crack in one of the bones in his foot. It was a remarkable answer to prayer, but what happened next that evening was just as unusual. This group of teenagers, not normally noted for their enthusiasm in worship and prayer, wanted to do just that. So we did, for about an hour and a half. Many of them were deeply touched by the Lord's Spirit in beautiful ways as we gave thanks to the One who had been so good to us all.

As I reflected on the whole series of events, I realised the key was the change which went on in many of their hearts as we dealt with the relational issues. It restored and enhanced the culture of openness to God's love. The robber of their blessing had been identified and put in his place. Then, by applying the simple principles of repentance and forgiveness in ways which were appropriate to the context, love was demonstrated to all concerned, especially the lad with the broken bone. There were no villains, there was no punishment, but there was transformation.

Do you remember the large ferny plant in the garden centre café from the last chapter? It relied on a carefully regulated climate to grow and flourish. Teachers who know Jesus, and have their internal climates controlled by His love, can bring the same influence to the climates around them, and when we see this happening it brings transformation to our classes and pupils.

To think about – can you imagine God doing unusual and wonderful things in your classes? What could they be?

Bad Days

It would be a great mistake if I communicated in such a way that you thought I was saying we should all be seeing dramatic change on a continual basis. My experience has been of a lot of days of simply doing my job. Teaching my lessons, marking work, doing playground duty, going to staff meetings, getting ready for the next day. There is a routine to what we do as teachers, but with it, a rhythm, the rhythm of the day, the week, the term, the year. This rhythmic routine helps us to maintain a sense of direction and purpose, and allows us to keep moving forward when we are not seeing great developments day in and day out.

Until something throws a spanner in the works, and we have a bad day.

Spanners can come from all directions but the hardest ones to deal with are the ones we throw ourselves, when we make mistakes. I feel I can speak with some authority here, as I have done this far too often.

I'm not planning to tell you about them all, or even some. I'm not proud of them, I'm simply grateful for a redemptive God who loves me enough, and is good enough to rescue me from my own ineptitude and foolishness. I'm also grateful for friends and colleagues who have loved me more than I have deserved, and forgiven me more times than I have realised.

So let's just accept I've blown it often enough to learn some valuable lessons, and whilst I know it is entirely your choice to make your own mistakes, without any help from me at all, I'd still like to share some of the lessons I've learned with you. In doing so I hope to show you how I deal with bad days.

Lesson One: don't take yourself too seriously. This piece of wisdom was given me many years ago by a man I respected greatly. Despite this it took me many more years to take it to heart. One time when I was in the aftermath of a work-based mess I had caused, I was still finding it hard to forgive myself, and I think this was because I was overestimating my importance in the situation. This can be a real barrier to freedom for many and it was for me at the time. As far as was possible in the circumstances, I had been through a process of honesty about what had happened, and restorative discussion with those involved. The problem was, my internal conversation was not helping me at all. I allowed myself to listen to the whispering accusations which were bouncing around my thoughts. It reached a kind of breaking point one day when I simply had to get to a phone, yes it was pre-mobiles, to call up one of the people involved and ask again if everything was at peace between us. Thankfully it was, but the internal pressure I was experiencing had built to such a degree it needed releasing somehow.

The phone call helped in the short term but didn't deal with the underlying issue, which was much more to do with my personal understanding of forgiveness. I wasn't allowing myself to properly receive God's forgiveness, and this was predominately because I thought my mistake, my sin, was so serious I deserved to suffer for it more than God intended. I was taking myself too seriously and imagining the whole of God's plan had been thrown into jeopardy by my actions.

I've since learned more about what the writer of Hebrews meant by, 'For by that one offering he forever made perfect those who are being made holy.' (Hebrews 10:14). What this reinforces, which is a central theme of the whole of the Bible, is this: under a covenant made through Jesus' sacrifice, there is no further punishment necessary for the sins we commit. This is not to say there won't ever be consequences from our actions; not at all, but there is no excuse for beating ourselves up simply because we messed up again. All this does is feed our own inverted sense of self-importance, which is just a fancy name for pride. It can almost feel virtuous to do it, but trying to add to the work of the cross does not help us draw any closer to God, because we are not acknowledging Jesus as the only source of forgiveness, help and restoration.

I've never found pride very helpful to me at all, especially in the light of God 'opposing the proud but giving grace to the humble' (James 4:6). So my advice is this, watch out for it, because it won't do anything good for you.

Lesson Two is related and it's this: I had to learn to really listen to other people and to do this well. I had to learn more about humility. This came as a bit of a surprise to me as I thought I was ever so humble. When I was at PE College I had a swimming tutor who was a fellow believer. This was unusual as it was not a Christian institution, but what was unfortunate was she and I did not get on especially well. This became a particular problem when I was applying to take a gap year after college with Youth for Christ, because I didn't have many people to choose from to ask for a reference. I asked her, and in my interview with YFC I was given some feedback from my reference, which was apparently giving the impression, 'He doesn't suffer fools lightly'. To be honest it was a fair assessment at the time, and I had the good sense not to try and disown it, but it took me many years to appreciate the value of such observations by other people.

Think about this for a moment. If we can't take on board comments from others which have truth in them, whether they like us or not, how can we help our pupils to do the same? Feedback is essential to learning, but as we grow older we recognise not everyone gives it helpfully. We need to find people who will help us reflect on these types of issues honestly and lovingly. We are involved in the business of helping our pupils grow and develop, so we have to entrust ourselves to the same process.

Lesson Three is where the rubber hits the road: can we decide on and make changes to our attitudes and behaviour which will show we have learned from our errors? I have put this question to more pupils than I can remember, but sometimes I have had to ask myself the same thing. Currently there is a TV advertising campaign running for a slimming product. The well-known lady fronting the whole thing does not look as if she especially needs the product, but you never can tell. The slogan is 'Change one thing'. It's good advice. I do not succeed when I try to change everything in my life, but when I make one alteration and work at it, I have more success.

For most teachers life is pressurised enough, isn't it? When we add to it the dimension of being one of just a few Christians in our school, or perhaps the only one as far as we are aware, our perception of what is at stake rises. We can end up putting ourselves under far more pressure than is good or necessary for us, and I think this results in an incorrect view of God, His purpose and our place in it.

We need to remember where our desire to serve and love the Lord comes from in the first place. From Him, right? If He had not looked for us initially, we would never have responded. He has always been infinitely more zealous to show His love and life to everyone than we could ever demonstrate. The fact that He chooses to use weak and flawed people is wonderful and we should never lose sight of it, but it doesn't all depend on us, which means we can relax and rejoice in His power and goodness.

So when you feel the spanner has been well and truly thrown, check through your feelings to see if you are looking at the situation with the wrong perspective. If you are, find a way, and some help if necessary, to access God's perspective. It's always better.

To think about – how do you manage yourself through mistakes? Are you getting better at it?

Thank You

I was at the end of a long project which had involved a lot of hard work. The idea for this venture had formed in me about eighteen months previously when I proposed it in a staff meeting. The scheme wasn't exactly dismissed, but the general response was, "Great idea Graham, but it's just too difficult to make it happen". At the end of the meeting a colleague commiserated with me by saying how sorry they were the idea wasn't going to become reality. I simply responded by saying, in true Hollywood hero style, 'It isn't over yet'.

Eighteen months later I was sitting in the playground of another school in a very deprived situation, watching my pupils loving and serving others and I had such a profound sense of gratitude. These were ordinary pupils who had gone far beyond what they had believed possible. Many of them lacked confidence in themselves and their abilities, many of them had never worked in this type of setting with the simple skills they had acquired.

Despite all of this, they had overcome significant obstacles and grown in their capacity to operate in an idea which had grown in their imaginations. If I had been looking for proven numbers of pupils making a commitment to follow Jesus, I would not have found much evidence of success. What I did see, however, was a group of young people who had begun to see greater possibilities for themselves. Possibilities of greater value than examination success, or the latest version of the iPhone.

As I sat there, I heard something I was not aware I had heard before. I heard the Lord say, 'Thank you'.

It broke me, I simply sat there and wept. I wept because I could feel His grace flooding through me and in response, my own love and gratitude overflowed back to Him.

This was not in a worship meeting, though it was worship. It was not in a celebrating crowd of thousands, though I believe there were thousands in Heaven celebrating with me. It was not in a church building, conference hall or festival marquee, it was in a very run-down playground next to a school building in desperate need of serious attention, but it was drawing the attention of Heaven at that moment.

The experience was profoundly moving, and still is as I write this, and it came about because I simply wanted to do my best as a teacher.

I am certain it's what you desire too.

If you find yourself agreeing with this, then please know that your Heavenly Father says, 'Thank you'.

Thank you for persevering day after day with your responsibilities because you have a desire to love your pupils through them continually. Thank you for going the extra mile again and again and again. Thank you for seeking the best for your pupils, their families and your colleagues whatever the difficulties and setbacks. Thank you for representing Jesus so well and for presenting His love and grace to everyone you encounter, whether you have felt like it or not. Thank you for praying for the people around you, and for wanting them to know more of the Father's love than they do. Thank you for listening to the Spirit, and for trying to find ways to follow His lead. Thank you for doing your best, even when you didn't believe your best was good enough.

I believe your Heavenly Father says, 'Thank you, precious child'.

To think about — take time and make space to hear the Lord say,
'Thank you'

Printed in Poland
by Amazon Fulfillment
Poland Sp. z o.o., Wrocław

58317037R10076